PASTOR—

This gift book is in appreciation for.
your fellowship in the World Literature
Crusade Radio Missionary Convention.

Oswald J. Smith

THE MESSAGE OF HOPE

THE MESSAGE OF HOPE

BY

OSWALD J. SMITH, Litt.D.

*Founder and Minister of Missions of
The Peoples Church, Toronto*

Foreword by
Dr. HENRY GRUBE

London
MARSHALL, MORGAN & SCOTT
Edinburgh

LONDON
MARSHALL, MORGAN AND SCOTT, LTD.
I–5 PORTPOOL LANE
HOLBORN, E.C.I

AUSTRALIA AND NEW ZEALAND
II7–II9 BURWOOD ROAD
MELBOURNE, E.I3

SOUTH AFRICA
P.O. BOX I720, STURK'S BUILDINGS
CAPE TOWN

CANADA
EVANGELICAL PUBLISHERS
24I YONGE STREET
TORONTO

THE PEOPLES CHURCH
374 SHEPPARD AVE. EAST
WILLOWDALE
ONTARIO

U.S.A.
CHRISTIAN LITERATURE CRUSADE
FORT WASHINGTON
PENNSYLVANIA

MADE AND PRINTED IN GREAT BRITAIN BY PURNELL AND SONS, LTD.
PAULTON (SOMERSET) AND LONDON

FOREWORD

In the summer of 1934 I realized what it meant to have Truth grip the heart and dominate the mind. I had been saved only a few years when a friend gave me a copy of a book written by Dr. Oswald J. Smith. I read the book at one sitting. Its message strengthened my faith. I read it again. I saw truths I had never seen before. In two weeks I had read the book three times. I made outlines of the chapter subjects, and preached the message of the book everywhere I went. That was twenty years ago. Today I still preach the same message of that book. It moulded my ministry. It typed my teaching. It established me in the fundamentals of the Faith.

Every Christian worker should read Dr. Smith's message on "God's Plan for Leadership" (now in his book *The Challenge of Life*), in which he makes clear the vital truth that God, when He wanted something done, chose a man, and placed him at the head of His people who were told to follow and obey his leadership. In the chapter on "Can Organized Religion Survive?" (in *The Battle For Truth*) Dr. Smith clearly points out the basic difference between Religion and Christianity. He shows that in Religion man works for God, but in the message of Christ we see God working for man. In the various religions of the world men are taught they must make promises to God in order to be saved, but in the Word of God we are shown that Salvation comes by taking and believing the promises God has made to us. So in these days, as well as when the book was first written twenty years ago, the message is greatly needed.

Today Dr. Smith is known for his ministry in foreign missions. He is recognized as one of the world's leading authorities on the motives and methods of world evangelism. He has proven his ability as an executive by the way he has managed the local ministry of The Peoples Church, as well as the way he has directed the activities of The Peoples Missionary Society.

Because he stresses Missions and Evangelism many have overlooked the fact that Dr. Smith is a student of the Word of God. He has that rare gift of being able to combine the message of an evangelist and a teacher. True, his basic appeal is to enlist volunteers for the mission field and win souls to Christ, but he bases his message and his ministry on the great doctrinal truths of the Word of God.

Dr. Smith has the rare gift of expounding the Word. There is nothing he enjoys more than preaching expository sermons. Throughout his ministry he has written on and proclaimed the great cardinal doctrines of the Christian Faith. This book is no exception. May it prove a blessing to both saint and sinner as it magnifies the Written and the Living Word.

H. G.

Mobile,
Alabama.

CONTENTS

GOD UNDERSTANDS

Oswald J. Smith

B. D. Ackley

Slowly, with expression

1. God un-der-stands your sor-row, He sees the fall-ing tear,
2. God un-der-stands your heart-ache, He knows the bit-ter pain;
3. God un-der-stands your weak-ness, He knows the tempt-er's pow'r;

And whis-pers, "I am with thee," Then fal-ter not, nor fear.
O, trust Him in the dark-ness, You can-not trust in vain.
And He will walk be-side you How-ev-er dark the hour.

REFRAIN

He un-der-stands your long-ing, Your deep-est grief He shares;

Then let Him bear your bur-den, He un-der-stands, and cares.

CHAPTER I

THE MESSAGE OF EASTER

WHEN I was in Ancient Russia I attended an Easter service which was held at midnight in a Greek Orthodox Church.

As the priests, after a long ceremony in which they marched three times around the church in search of the body of Christ, re-entered, they cried out, "Christ is risen". And the people, bowing in adoration, exclaimed, "He is risen, indeed!"

That, in a word, is the Easter message. And it is because of the resurrection that we look forward with hope to the day when we, too, shall rise.

The reality of Christ's resurrection is easily proved. It rests upon the best attested facts in history.

First of all, we have four separate and independent accounts. On the surface there are variations, but a close-up study reveals the harmony that exists between them all.

Admittedly, they must be true or false. They must have been made up independently or together. There is no other alternative.

That they could not have been made up independently is demonstrated by the fact that the harmony is by far too complete. They are too much alike. This could not have been had they been manufactured by individuals who had nothing whatever to do with each other.

On the other hand, there could have been no consultation, no previous agreement or understanding, simply because there are too many differences. Had the writers collaborated, they would have seen to it that there were no variations. Therefore, they were not made up at all, either independently or in consultation. They are true statements of facts. The resurrection of the Lord Jesus Christ was presented by each one as he himself saw it. Thus they are authentic.

In the second place, a careful study of the resurrection reveals the fact that most of the accounts were written by eye-witnesses. Those who wrote saw with their own eyes the risen Christ.

The story is related simply and with no attempt to colour it or exaggerate. One tells what another omits. This accounts for the apparent differences.

Had they made it up years later they would certainly have represented Him as appearing to His enemies and confounding them. That would have been the natural climax to the story. No writer of fiction would have thought of anything else. What an opportunity they missed! But the fact is, He appeared only to His disciples.

In the third place, even infidels admit that His disciples believed He had risen.

Renan, for instance, said that it was a hallucinated woman who gave the world a resurrected God. But that is impossible and absurd, for there was a Matthew and a Thomas to convince and a Paul to convert.

Strauss declares that His appearances were visionary. But the eleven and the five hundred could not have had the same vision.

Others insist that He never died. What, then, of the "water and blood"? How account for it if He were not dead?

Moreover, His enemies guarded His body, and if He had only fainted He would have been weak and would not have been able to escape from the tomb.

Last of all, Jesus Himself would have been an impostor. He stated that He would rise and He did. After His resurrection He declared that He had risen from the dead. If His word was untrue, then He was a liar and unworthy of our allegiance.

The resurrection of the Lord Jesus Christ, as I have said, is one of the best attested facts in history. There are hundreds of historical events that do not have nearly as many witnesses. Just think, there were fourteen groups that saw Him alive after His death:

1. Mary Magdalene at the tomb.
2. The women.
3. Peter.
4. The two disciples at Emmaus.
5. The disciples in the upper room.
6. The disciples with Thomas.
7. The disciples on the shore of Galilee.
8. The eleven on a mountain.
9. The five hundred brethren at once.
10. James.
11. The disciples on Olivet at the Ascension.
12. Stephen at his martyrdom.
13. Paul on the road to Damascus.
14. John on Patmos.

Now, some of these witnesses saw Him, not once, but several times. How could they have been mistaken?

The fact that many of them died for their testimony shows their reliability. Men do not die for nothing, not voluntarily. Yet these men and women gladly suffered martyrdom rather than deny their Risen Lord.

Had these witnesses been false their enemies would have produced contrary evidence. Whereas, the best thing they could do was to spread the story about the disciples having stolen His body while the soldiers were asleep.

But note, if you will, that that was the soldiers' story. They were asleep, so they said, and while sleeping they saw the disciples come and steal His body. Strange things to see when one is asleep.

And think of a Roman guard being asleep, every man. Impossible!

On the other hand, how are you going to harmonize the theft with the order in which the graveclothes were found, the handkerchief, etc.? When thieves break in they leave everything in confusion. But not so in the tomb of Jesus. The handkerchief was folded neatly and laid in a place by itself. The graveclothes were left in an orderly condition. There were no signs of fright and haste as there would have been had the nervous disciples attempted to take His body from the tomb.

You must never forget the fear of His followers. They were afraid. In fact, they all forsook Him and fled. They had lost every atom of courage. And hence they would have been the last ones in the world to attempt the theft of a dead body from a tomb surrounded by a Roman guard.

In any case, how are you going to account for the miraculous change from fear to courage, and even boldness, as a result of His resurrection? Had they stolen His body they would have remained in hiding. But the fact that they came out boldly, openly and publicly and proclaimed His resurrection, even going so far as to accuse the Jews and the members of the Sanhedrin of murdering Him, proves conclusively that they had nothing to do with His reappearance.

No, His enemies produced no contrary evidence. They had nothing to say. Their explanations were childish, absurd and impossible. But had He not risen, how quickly they would have proven it.

The founders of all the world's religions have died, nor

have they ever been resurrected. Christ and Christ alone arose.

When Talleyrand, the great agnostic, wanted to found a new religion, and finding it hard going, asked counsel of the King of France, he received this answer: "Go and be crucified, and on the third day rise again and men will believe in your religion."

Yes, Jesus Christ rose from the dead, and because He rose, we, too, shall rise, for His resurrection is the guarantee of ours.

But, some will ask, with what bodies will we appear? That question was asked and answered by Paul long ago. We shall be like Him, we are told. And if we can discover the kind of body He had we will know something of the body that we too shall have on that Day.

A Spiritual Body

First of all, it is clear from the Word of God that our Lord was given a spiritual body. Then we, too, will have spiritual bodies. And what is a spiritual body? A body that is not subject to natural law.

After our Lord was raised from the dead He could not be kept in or out by gates and bars. When the disciples were gathered together, first without Thomas and then with him, Jesus suddenly appeared in their midst. How He got in no one knew. But there He was. And as He ate before them and showed them His hands and His side, they knew that it was Jesus Himself, and that in spite of the fact that the doors were shut He came in.

So will it be with us. Walls will form no barrier. We will be able to pass through them as easily as we now pass through the air we breathe. Gravitation will no longer be able to hold us. To step off a high building will be perfectly safe. Without laboriously climbing stairs we will be able to ascend of our own free will.

Space will be annihilated. We will be able to go from place to place unhindered and unhampered, and at any speed we choose. Distance will mean nothing. If we desire to speed from planet to planet it will be easy, for we shall have spiritual bodies, and a spiritual body is not subject to natural law.

A Powerful Body

In the second place, our Lord was given a powerful body. And we, too, shall have powerful bodies. Today we grow tired and weary. Oft-times we are unable to complete our tasks, or to do the work that we long to do. We become weary and exhausted. We have to rest. Sleep is necessary. Sometimes a long vacation is inevitable, and all because these bodies of ours wear out.

But with our resurrection body we will never know fatigue. Never again will we say, "I am tired." All weariness will be gone. Our bodies will never become exhausted. Sleep will not be necessary. Never again will we be compelled to stop and rest. With our resurrection bodies we will have all the endurance necessary for our work. How wonderful it will be never to be weary again.

An Immortal Body

Then, too, our Lord had an immortal body, a body that could never die. And we, too, shall have such a body. There can be no death in Heaven. The Bible tells us that the last enemy that shall be destroyed is death. So there will be no death. Never again will we have to die. There will be no funerals in Heaven, no crêpe on the doors. Cemeteries will be unknown. The work of the undertaker will be over. Never again will there be a separation. Death will be no more. Immortal bodies cannot die.

An Incorruptible Body

But again, our Lord had an incorruptible body. And our resurrection bodies will also be incorruptible. Every seven years these bodies of ours undergo a change. They have to be renewed from time to time. They are continually corrupting. But in the resurrection life corruption will be unknown. Our bodies will last forever. There will be no decay, no corruption. Corruption belongs to earth. We shall have incorruptible bodies.

A Glorified Body

Lastly, our Lord was given a glorified body, a body so glorious that it outshone the glory of the sun. And we, too, shall have glorified bodies, bodies infinitely brighter than the noon-day sun.

We are given a glimpse of such a body on the Mount of Transfiguration, where, it is said, the very raiment of our Lord glistened and shone as He was transfigured in the presence of His disciples. Thus will we shine through all Eternity.

They that turn many to righteousness, says God, shall shine as the stars for ever and ever. The brightest sun ever created will look dim in contrast to the brightness of our glorified bodies. Light unapproachable by human beings will be ours.

Like Him

How beautiful we will be in that day it is impossible to say. All we know is that we are told that we will be like Him. He died when He was about thirty-three years of age. Hence we will be eternally young. Wrinkles, therefore, will be gone and the beauty of youth, glorified by the resurrection, restored.

We shall be changed, we are told, changed into His likeness, and with those who have gone before, caught up to meet the Lord in the air. And, oh, what a change! It is to this we look forward as we celebrate another Easter.

And when will it take place? When are we to receive our resurrection bodies? When are all these promises to be fulfilled? At the time of the Second Coming of our Lord. It will be when He returns. No one until then will be resurrected. Today God's people await that morn. The trumpet shall sound. The dead in Christ will be raised, living believers changed, and both caught up to meet the Lord in the air.

Then will come the Bema judgment, the day of rewards, and the marriage supper of the Lamb; after that our reign with Christ for a thousand years, and then, endless Eternity.

Oh, what a prospect! No wonder we glory in Easter. Not only does it remind us of the resurrection of our Lord, but, as already stated, it speaks to us of our own resurrection and the glories that await us. Glad Easter Day!

CHAPTER II

WORLDLY WISDOM OR DIVINE POWER

PAUL'S admonition to the Philippians, "Have no confidence in the flesh," was never more needed than now. Great and grave dangers face the Church of Jesus Christ. More and more men are depending on education and worldly wisdom instead of on God's Dynamic.

Here, for instance, is a man who wants to argue:

"Are you a Christian?" you enquire.

"Well," answers the man, "I would like to know where Cain got his wife."

"But, my friend, is your soul saved? I am interested in your soul's salvation."

"How do you think a man should be baptized?"

"I will deal with that after you accept Christ. It really makes no difference until you are saved."

"Do you believe what the Bible says about the sun standing still?"

"My friend, I believe you need Jesus and I want to urge you to accept Him now."

"But which church should a man join?"

"No church until he knows Christ. Will you receive Him?"

Thus you keep him to the point and compel him to face the issue, for the moment you commence to answer his questions he will get you into an argument. But by dealing only with the question of his soul's salvation, the Spirit of God will, sooner or later, produce conviction.

A New Convert

I remember a story about a very young convert. He knew nothing regarding personal work, but he did know one passage of Scripture. Approaching an infidel he invited him to Christ.

"But I don't believe in Christ," said the infidel.

"Well," responded the new convert, "the Bible says, 'He that believeth not shall be damned.' "

"But I don't believe the Bible either," responded the infidel.

"That doesn't change it," answered the other, "because God declares that, 'He that believeth not shall be damned.' "

"God! Haven't I told you I don't believe in God? I tell you there is no God," exclaimed the infidel, his wrath rising.

"And again I say," quietly responded the new convert, "that 'He that believeth not shall be damned.' "

Picking up his hat, the infidel, in a fury of rage, pushed him aside, and left the building, cursing and swearing as he went. The young convert, somewhat disappointed and humiliated, offered an earnest prayer, lamenting his lack of knowledge, and asking the Spirit of God to work. And He did. The man went home and to bed, but not to sleep. Hour after hour he tossed restlessly from side to side. All his old-time arguments upon which he had prided himself he went over one by one. Yet every now and then he would hear those solemn words: "He that believeth not shall be damned." At last, unable to bear it longer, he climbed out of bed, fell on his knees and prayed, "O God, if there be a God, save me. Reveal Thy Son to me and help me to believe." And before long he was rejoicing in Christ.

The Word, you see, is quick and powerful. It is

sharper than any two-edged sword. And it alone God has promised to bless and use. Not your arguments, but His Word. It, says God, shall prosper. Oh, then, preach the Word.

Education is not a necessity. Even a knowledge of the language is not essential. Interpretation can be effective. Brainerd's interpreter was a drunken Indian, yet God blessed His Word until the Indians were stung with conviction.

Paul's Ministry

"And I, brethren, when I came to you, came not with excellency of speech or of wisdom, declaring unto you the testimony of God."

Think of it! Paul, educated, trained, talented. Yet he made no effort to be eloquent, for well he knew that oratory was powerless to produce conviction and repentance. No, nor wisdom. All his great learning he cast aside.

"For I determined not to know anything among you, save Jesus Christ, and Him crucified!" (1 Cor. 2: 2). What a confession! No wonder God so mightily used him. For here was one who had "no confidence in the flesh." In other words, he hid, as it were, his great learning and became in the sight of the people an ignoramus. He determined to know—how much? A little? No, nothing. And yet—everything. One man, but He the God-Man, Christ Jesus. And then he adds: "Him crucified," a death that carried with it the deepest disgrace known. Oh, how the Cross was despised! Yet Paul determined to put it in, for He knew its power. And the Cross is the heart, the dynamite of the Gospel. Let us never forget it, for remember, there is no Gospel without a Cross. Paul knew God's dynamite and he used it, for he wanted results, and he got them. "For the preaching of the Cross is to them that perish foolishness; but unto us which are saved it is the power of God" (1 Cor. 1: 18).

"And my speech and my preaching was not with enticing words of man's wisdom, but in demonstration of the Spirit and of power" (1 Cor. 2: 4).

Now we have the secret. No words of worldly allurement. Nothing of the wisdom and learning of man. That is all cast aside. Reliance is entirely upon the Holy Spirit. He is the Demonstrator of what the Gospel will do.

"But the natural man receiveth not the things of the Spirit of God: for they are foolishness unto him; neither can he know them, because they are spiritually discerned."

The natural, the unregenerate man, you see, cannot intellectually understand the things of God, because they are in a realm with which he is entirely unacquainted. With the natural he is familiar and at home, but to the spiritual he is a stranger. Hence the utter uselessness of seeking to convince him by human reasoning.

"For after that in the wisdom of God the world by wisdom knew not God, it pleased God by the foolishness of preaching to save them that believe. God hath chosen the foolish things of the world to confound the wise; and God hath chosen the weak things of the world to confound the things which are mighty; and base things of the world, and things which are despised, hath God chosen, yea, and things which are not, to bring to naught things that are: that no flesh should glory in His presence" (1 Cor. 1: 21, 27-29).

Oh, how plain, how unmistakable! The world by all its accumulated wisdom, declares Paul, failed to know God. Salvation, he continues, results from something that any believer can do—preach. Note God's choice— the foolish, the weak, the base, the despised, the nothings. And with these, these who "have no confidence in the flesh," He confounds the wise, the mighty, the worldly somebodies. And so we glory in Him and in Him alone. Blessed be God!

The Gospel

"For I am not ashamed of the Gospel of Christ: for it is the power of God unto salvation to every one that believeth" (Rom. 1: 16).

The Gospel, not your wisdom, training, education, talents or gifts; the *Gospel* is the power, the dynamic of God. Oh, my brethren, let me appeal to you. Let not worldly wisdom blind you to the glories of the Gospel, nor deceive you as to its power.

"Go ye into all the world and preach the Gospel to every creature." Preach it to the high and to the low. Preach it to the rich and to the poor. Preach it to the old and to the young. Preach it to the learned and to the ignorant, to royalty and to peasant alike, for all are equal in God's sight. "All have sinned," therefore all need a Saviour.

"So shall my Word be that goeth forth out of My mouth: *it* shall not return unto Me void, but *it* shall accomplish that which I please, and *it* shall prosper in the thing whereto I sent it" (Isa. 55: 11).

CHAPTER III

THE SHADOW OF THE CROSS

THE internal evidence for the claims of Jesus Christ are absolutely irrefutable. Again and again the shadow of the cross falls across His pathway and proves conclusively that He knew the end from the beginning. If He was not the Son of God, if He was not what He claimed to be, then how did He know?

Infidels, atheists, and agnostics never have and never can refute His claims. No mere man has ever been able to describe his own death; but this Man—the God Man—did. He knew exactly what was going to happen. How, I ask, is the unbeliever going to explain it?

The Gospel of Matthew

In Matthew 16: 21 we behold the shadow of the cross for the first time during His earthly ministry. This verse reads as follows:

> "From that time forth began Jesus to shew unto His disciples, how that He must go unto Jerusalem, and suffer many things of the elders and chief priests and scribes, and be killed, and be raised again the third day."

Here was Jesus in the very midst of His ministry, long before it happened, telling His disciples exactly how it would all end. It was to be in Jerusalem. Could any mere man name the city, village, or town in which he would die? Jesus did. He named Jerusalem. It might have been Nazareth, or Samaria, or Bethlehem, or Jericho, or any other of the hundreds of villages and cities of Palestine; but He named only one—Jerusalem. How, I ask, did He know?

He said He would suffer many things of the elders, chief priests, and scribes. How did He know that? He stated that He would be killed—not, mark you, that He would die a natural death—He was to be executed and He knew it. If He was not the Son of God, if He did not possess omniscience, then how are we going to explain the accurate information which He gave to His disciples?

Moreover, He said that He would be raised again. Could any ordinary man have made such a claim? Could you, could I? Furthermore, He said it would be on the third day. He knew the exact day it would happen. He was to be resurrected; He knew it and He told it long before it happened. Later on it took place exactly as He said it would. How, I ask, did He know? There is but one explanation. He must have been what He said He was, very God of very God.

But again the same shadow falls across His pathway. Look at Matthew 17: 22, 23:

> "The Son of man shall be betrayed into the hands of men: and they shall kill Him, and the third day He shall be raised again."

Here He tells His disciples that He is to be betrayed. How did He know that? He states again that He is to be killed and also that He would be raised on the third day. These predictions, as everyone knows, were literally fulfilled. He *was* betrayed. Let the sceptic explain it, if he can. If Christ was only human, then He could not have known, for no mere man has ever known the details regarding his death.

The Gospel of Mark

Turn now to Mark 8: 31. Here again we see the shadow of the cross:

> "He began to teach them, that the Son of man must suffer many things, and be rejected of the elders, and of the chief priests, and scribes, and be killed, and after three days rise again."

Mark says that He spoke quite openly. Apparently He had no fear of contradiction. He knew in advance that He would suffer many things, that He would be rejected, that it would be the elders, chief priests, and scribes who would be responsible, and that He would be killed, namely, executed. He knew also that within three days He would rise again. Could He have known had He been but a man? Most certainly not. For no man knows the end from the beginning. Christ did: and He knew because He was God, God manifested in the flesh. What has the unbeliever to say?

But again the shadow appears. Look at Mark 9: 9, 10. Here He speaks of rising from the dead, and the disciples, Mark says, were unable to understand him.

In Mark 9: 31 we have this statement:

> "The Son of man is delivered into the hands of men, and they shall kill Him; and after that He is killed, He shall rise the third day."

There, again, He predicts in detail His death and resurrection, though the disciples did not understand.

The last passage in Mark is found in the tenth chapter, verses 33 and 34:

"Behold, we go up to Jerusalem; and the Son of man shall be delivered unto the chief priests, and unto the scribes; and they shall condemn Him to death, and shall deliver Him to the Gentiles: and they shall mock Him and shall scourge Him, and shall spit upon Him, and shall kill Him: and the third day He shall rise again."

Now here are a number of new facts, minute details, that only one who was omniscient could have revealed. The agnostic will have a hard time explaining these details. Neither Modernism nor Higher Criticism will have an answer. Either Christ was what He claimed to be—God manifested in the flesh—or else there is no explanation.

He said it would happen in Jerusalem. We had that before. He stated that He would be delivered to the authorities; that He would be condemned to death and then handed over to the Gentiles. That, of course, is exactly what happened. He was first condemned by the Jews and then sent to Pilate. But how did He know that His trial would proceed along these lines? He said He would be mocked; He was. He stated that they would scourge Him; they did. Then He gave again the information He had given before, namely, that He would be killed and on the third day resurrected.

But now note one added detail, a detail so insignificant yet so important that it cannot be overlooked. He said they would spit on Him. How did He know that? Here we have a mere detail; not only is He to be killed, He is to be spit upon; and long before it happens He tells His disciples all about it. Surely He was what He claimed to be—the Son of the living God. He knew the end from

the beginning, He could not be surprised, He was able to
foretell even in detail the agonies through which He would
pass.

The Gospel of Luke

We turn now to Luke and here again we behold the
shadow of the cross. First of all Luke 9: 31. Here His
heavenly visitors, Moses and Elijah, talked with Him
about the death He was to die at Jerusalem. Hence it
could be no surprise when it came.

In Luke 18: 31–33 we have these words:

"Behold, we go up to Jerusalem, and all things that
are written by the prophets concerning the Son of man
shall be accomplished. For He shall be delivered unto
the Gentiles, and shall be mocked, and spitefully entreated, and spitted on: and they shall scourge Him,
and put Him to death: and the third day He shall rise
again." (See 9: 44 and 17: 25.)

Here are several new facts which He imparted to His
twelve disciples. He recognizes that the prophets of the
Old Testament Scriptures had written about Him hundreds
of years before and He states that everything written
would be accomplished. Then He gives a number of
details. He speaks once more of being mocked, spitefully
entreated, and spat upon. He says again that He would
be scourged, put to death, and raised the third day.

In Luke 22: 19, 20 He breaks the bread and says:
"This is my body which is given for you." He takes the
cup and declares, "This cup is the new testament in my
blood, which is shed for you." Thus He speaks of His
body being broken and His blood being shed.

The last passage in Luke is found in chapter 24, verse
7, 8:

"The Son of man must be delivered into the hands of sinful men, and be crucified, and the third day rise again."

Here we have a statement after His resurrection, reminding the disciples of what He had said before He had died, as if to say, "Didn't He tell you so? Don't you remember what He said? Can't you recall His statements? Why are you so blind? Months before it happened He told you all these things that have now taken place. Why didn't you believe Him? Do you realize now that He was no mere man? Do you now admit His Deity? Be not faithless, but believing."

The Gospel of John

Having dealt with the Synoptics, let us turn now to the Gospel of John and glance at a number of important passages:

"Destroy this temple, and in three days I will raise it up" (John 2: 19). Verse 21 says that He referred to His body. Well, they destroyed it, but in three days it was raised again.

John 10: 11, 15, 17, 18.—In verse 11 He prophesied that He would give His life, and He did. In verse 15 He said He would "lay down" His life, and He did. In verse 17 He adds that He would take it again, and in verse 18 declares that no one could take it from Him, that He had power both to lay it down and take it. That alone stamps Him with deity.

No mortal man can lay down His life of his own free will; he can be killed, but he cannot die when he wants to. Jesus did. While hanging on the cross He cried, "It is finished"; then He added, "Father, into thy hands I commend my spirit." After that the Word says "He gave up the ghost," or, as it is in the original, "He dismissed His spirit."

The soldiers broke the legs of the thieves because they were not dead, but when they came to Jesus they found He was dead already. He ought not to have died so quickly, and He would not have died when He did had He been an ordinary man. He being God, was able to die at will, and when He was ready He simply dismissed His spirit, and He was dead.

Likewise, on the third day He returned from Paradise, where He had gone with the thief, re-entered His cold, inanimate body, rose up and walked out of the sepulchre. He had the power to take the body He had laid down. No one else has ever had that power. Was He not divine? Was He not God? If not, then who was He?

"And I, if I be lifted up from the earth, will draw all men unto me. This He said, signifying what death He should die" (John 12: 32, 33). See John 8: 28.

Here, definitely long before it took place, He states that He is to die by crucifixion. He says again that He is to be lifted up. He knew He would be lifted up upon the cross. John plainly declares that He said this in order to describe the very manner of His death. It was to be death by crucifixion. If He was not God, how did He know it?

For the last time the shadow of the cross is seen in John 13: 1, where John says that Jesus knew that His hour had come and that He was about to depart out of the world unto His Father. He knew it, John says, knew the very hour, knew that the time had come to leave the world, knew that He was going to His Father. But how did He know? He knew because He was exactly what He claimed to be. He was God incarnate in flesh. Only God possesses omniscience.

Here, then, we see the shadow of the cross throughout His entire ministry. Again I point out that He was never surprised. Nothing happened that He did not expect. He knew everything. What has the unbeliever to say? In view of these facts, how can he ignore the claims of Christ?

We Must Meet Him

One of these days we shall all stand before this Christ of whom we have been speaking. He has made an appointment with us that we cannot evade. The God who was manifested in flesh is to be our Judge.

We have no excuse for our unbelief. We must come to the conclusion that He was what He said He was; and if that be so, then we must get ready to meet Him, for there is no escape.

Let me suggest that the doubter sit down and read again the passages I have listed; that he read them prayerfully, asking God to illuminate his darkened mind, that he may come to know the Christ who knows all about him, and who will some day call him to account; then let him open his heart and accept this Christ, whom he has so long rejected, as his own personal Saviour. He will then fall down before Him and cry with Thomas of old, "My Lord and my God."

CHAPTER IV

THE USE OF MEANS IN HEALING

GOD HEALS by both natural and supernatural means, gradually and instantaneously, as it pleases Him, human means not necessarily forming a barrier to Divine intervention.

In other words, it is simply a question of drawing the line. Everyone uses means of some kind. Certain drugs are harmful to the body. But God Himself has placed many simple remedies in the world which from time to time have been discovered by man and employed for the alleviation of human suffering. It does not seem plausible that such provision should be made unless it was intended for use. As to when and what means are to be employed must be determined by the believer according to the will of God. Guidance will be given in answer to earnest prayer.

Hudson Taylor

May I give here the testimony of the sainted founder of the China Inland Mission, J. Hudson Taylor? It is worthy of the closest study and is most illuminating, to say the least. He writes as follows:

"One thing was a great trouble to me. I was a very young believer, and had not sufficient faith in God to see Him in and through the use of means. I had felt it a duty to comply with the earnest wish of my beloved and honoured mother, and, for her sake, to procure a swimming-belt; but my heart had no rest until I had given it away. Then I had perfect peace. But, strange to say, I put several light things together, likely to keep me afloat in case of accident, without any thought of inconsistency or scruple. Ever since I have seen clearly the mistake I made—a mistake that is very common in these days, when erroneous teaching on faith-healing does much harm, misleading some as to the purposes of God, shaking the faith of others, and distressing the minds of many. The use of means ought not to lessen our faith in God; and our faith in God ought not to hinder our using whatever means He has given us for the accomplishment of His own purposes.

"For years after this I always took a swimming-belt with me, and never had any trouble about it; for the question had at last been settled for me, through the prayerful study of the Scriptures. God gave me then to see my mistake, probably to deliver me from a great deal of trouble on similar questions now so constantly raised. When in medical or surgical charge of any case, I have never thought of neglecting to ask God's guidance and blessing in the use of appropriate means, nor yet of omitting to give Him thanks for answered prayer and restored health. But to me it would appear as presumptuous and wrong to neglect the use of those measures which He Himself has put within our reach, as to neglect to take daily food, and suppose that life and health might be maintained by prayer alone."

A careful study of the miracles wrought in the Bible, so far as they are mentioned, will make it clear that in the majority of cases at least the disease or affliction was of an incurable nature, and thus absolutely beyond the help of man. Is it not true that God does what man cannot do? As long as simple and harmless remedies are able to meet the situation, should they not be employed unless God leads otherwise? But what are we to do when we are face to face with an incurable disease? Are all such to be given up as hopeless, simply because man has no remedy, no means by which to effect a cure? Most assuredly not. When all else has failed God is still able.

If we are to rule out the use of means entirely, then we will be forced to give a new interpretation to Philippians 4: 19 and to other similar passages. The promise reads: "My God shall supply all your need." Is the farmer, therefore, to simply sit down and wait for the fulfilment of this promise in a purely supernatural manner, or must he not employ means? Certainly God could meet all his need without an effort on his part, but such is not the Divine plan. He must clear the land, plough the ground, sow his grain, cultivate and care for it. In a word, he must do everything that he can do, and then when he arrives at the place where human means fail and the supernatural must be employed, God comes on the scene, sends the rain and the sun, causes the grain to grow and ripen, and thus the farmer's needs are supplied.

Now God declares: "I am the Lord that healeth thee" (Exod. 15: 26), but should not this statement be taken in precisely the same way as Philippians 4: 19, "My God shall supply all your need"? As to how it is fulfilled rests with Him alone. He may lead the sick one to depend wholly upon supernatural means. But on the other hand He may guide to the use of some known remedy that will at once serve the purpose and bring healing on the natural plane.

John Wesley

John Wesley was a man of unusual faith, and many a time when no means were available he prayed, believed, and received immediate and miraculous answers for those afflicted. At one time he even prayed for the restoration of his horse, and God answered. Yet Wesley wrote an entire book on Remedies, and whenever means were available he employed them without hesitation.

I recall an incident of a very spiritual woman, an evangelist, who had taken the stand all her life that it was a sin to use remedies of any kind whatever. There came a time when she found herself sick; and in spite of the fact that she prayed and sought God most earnestly with many tears and was anointed by a man of faith, she failed to get deliverance. Many joined her in prayer and fasting but without avail.

Finally, after waiting upon the Lord for many days, there came to her an impression like a voice in her soul, saying: "I will heal you on the natural plane." "But, Lord," she exclaimed in amazement, "I have been preaching for years that it is a sin to use means of any kind. I would rather die than be healed through remedies." Well, she prayed on, but each time there came to her the same quiet word, and in spite of all she could do she still remained a very sick woman.

After battling in prayer until she was almost worn out, she began at last to ask God what she should do. He quickly brought to her mind the thought of a very simple remedy, and after a final struggle with herself, she yielded, surrendered her will absolutely to God and took what He had directed. In a few days she was better, and before long regained her strength and was enabled to continue her evangelistic work.

You see, God had to break her will, for on that one point she was unsurrendered. Having been once wonderfully healed in a supernatural way, she had concluded that God must always act as He had then, and thus through her teaching she had been leading people into bondage until many felt that every time they used means they were sinning against God. The only safe way is to seek God's will upon each occasion, and obediently

c

follow the light given. It is not ours to dictate, but to obey.

It would be just as sensible for Elijah to declare that since God had fed him at one time by ravens, he must always be fed in the same way.

I do not believe that the poultice of figs used on Hezekiah was merely typical or only for a sign. If ordered by God, then there must have been some healing virtue in it.

Paul's suggestion of grape juice as a substitute for the unhealthy waters of the East was surely wise counsel. How much more digestible and suitable for a man naturally delicate and weak! Of course, God could have made Timothy a big, robust giant. But then Timothy would have had natural strength, and would therefore have been independent of God.

Some people even wonder if it is right to diet, their argument being that God should so heal them that they could eat anything. What absurdity! God surely expects His servants to use common sense and know the things that are good for them and those which are harmful. Some can stand certain foods that would be absolutely ruinous to others.

Up until 1910 only one remedy had been discovered that would cure disease. Doctors treated the symptoms rather than the causes and then let nature do the healing. Since 1910 many wonder drugs have been discovered and now for the first time the germs that cause the disease can be destroyed. As a result, untold thousands have lived who before 1910 would have died. If God has enabled man to find such cures, is it not His will that they should be used?

Consistent in Everything

If means are not to be used, then we dare not wear glasses, even in old age. Yet according to the Bible there is a natural failing of the eyesight as the body becomes infirm, but such infirmity is not sickness. Isaac, you remember, had such dim eyesight that he could not tell his sons apart. And yet God nowhere rebukes him for it. Glasses might have meant much to him in his old age. Jacob was afflicted in the same way, and still he blessed the sons of Joseph. But if we are to be true to the position of "no means," we must lay aside eye-glasses. (See 1 Kings 14: 4.)

The same holds good regarding the teeth. It would be impossible to consult a dentist if remedies and means are to be ruled out. There could be no compromise.

Most certainly, the first missionaries went out to brave the African fever without quinine; but so many were the deaths that expedience demanded a new position.

There is scarcely a Mission Board to-day, however, that would think of prohibiting quinine. It is God's appointed remedy for malaria in the African jungles. To argue that it is a food is merely a dishonest evasion of the question. And if means are thus used in Africa, then it is absurd to maintain a different position at home. If the position of "no means" is right, it must be applied universally, under all conditions, and without any modification. To preach one thing and practise another is not honest.

In 2 Chronicles 16: 12, we read that "Asa sought not to the Lord, but to the physicians." Now the emphasis must be laid not on the latter phrase but upon the former. It was not because he went to the physicians that he died, but because of the fact that during the time of his disease he did not seek the Lord. Asa had back-slidden to a fearful degree, and in his backsliding he seemed to utterly ignore God.

Since Christ is our life and is therefore sufficient for spirit, soul and body, being able to supply all our needs (Phil. 4: 19)—physical, temporal and spiritual—it is therefore our privilege to have His life made manifest in our bodies or our mortal flesh, as well as in our spirit and soul, and to know Him as our Healer (Rom. 8: 11). Hence, being thus kept in health, we will have little or no need of human remedies (2 Cor. 4: 10, 11). Yet, should human means seem advisable, even an operation, we will not allow ourselves to be brought into bondage. Remember Ezekiel's leaves; they were for medicine (Ezek. 47: 12; Rev. 22: 2). We are free. But let us use our liberty to the glory of God.

CHAPTER V

HOW TO FACE SUFFERING

FROM far and near I have received letters in which just one note has been sounded, and that note—loneliness. During the years I have been broadcasting I have received hundreds of letters, many filled with confessions of heartache too sacred to mention. And these letters I am going to try to answer tonight.

Perhaps I may be able to say something to one and all that will bring comfort and consolation. My ministry must be characterized more and more by tenderness and love. Harshness, criticism, judging, and condemning, I leave to others. These letters, expressive of a thousand heartaches, have told me that nothing is more needed in these days of testing and trial than a sympathetic understanding of the burdens of others.

I seem to see you now—all who have written to me, as I close my eyes and talk to you over the air, for there you sit alone by your radio, and it is almost eleven o'clock. The lights are turned low. You listen. And, as my voice enters your room, you think of other days, days that are no more. No wonder the tear-drops fall. You are friendless, and in some cases, homeless. You live by yourself, utterly forsaken, and tonight, so disconsolate. Oh, how my heart aches for you as I think of you out there in Radio Land! Your life has been so hard, your trials so many, and your burdens so heavy, as you have struggled on—alone.

Once, perchance, you were loved. Someone cared for you. How bright the future looked! You were young then and love entwined itself around your heart. Love satisfied. For love, true love, is the greatest thing in the world. Love is eternal. I don't mean lust and passion. That is not love. Love is holy. Love is pure. Love is noble and true. Love never fails, God says. Love is worth more than all the millions and all the fame of earth. God pity you if you have never been loved. There is nothing like it in the universe.

You loved and you were loved. Such is the story that scores of you have told me in your letters. Then one day something happened. Love took wings and fled, and when it did you felt as though the sun had suddenly faded from the sky. The flowers bloomed no more, the birds ceased to sing, and all the world was dark. Sadly the letters were tied together and put away, and with them the little gifts and pictures, all so precious. For a while it seemed as though bitterness and resentment would fill your heart. But at last, as the years passed by, you turned to your work and tried to forget.

But to-night you are lonely, oh, so lonely! Again and again you find yourself repeating the almost sacred words:

> *"O for the touch of a vanished hand,*
> *And the sound of a voice that is still."*

But there is no answer, only a great silence. And soon now you will be old and grey. Already you are well on in middle life. Other friends have come and gone. You have made money. You have attained fame. Comforts surround you on every side. Other interests have claimed your attention. Yet to-night you are sad. Your heart aches. You ask why it happened, why you were disappointed.

Young people look up to you and envy you your place. They wonder how you succeeded. The real things in life don't mean much to them—not yet. They seek your honour. To achieve is their one ambition. Ah, how little they know of the cost, the struggle, the battle, the cross! How little they think of the trials, the heartaches, the disappointments! And you, how gladly you would give all up and live in obscurity, in poverty, if only you could go back.

The other day, so you tell me, you got out the faded bundle of letters. But you could not read them. You touched them, you gazed at the familiar handwriting. You read one or two of the postcards and a great lump rose in your throat. Tears welled to your eyes. And wrapping them up again, you put them away.

Next day, you continue, you tried once more. Your every thought was of the scenes of yore. Once again you saw a youthful smiling face, eyes that shone with love for you. You took out a little locket, a ring, a faded flower, a lock of hair, and kissed them, oh, so tenderly. How many things have happened since last you saw them! How the years have fled!

Then you read the letters, read them until you could read no more. The word "forever"—how often it occurred! "Your love may change; I am sure mine never will. I cannot live without you. I am yours forever," you read. "Forever yours." O fateful words! And then the plans for your home and the bright, happy future. Oh, what dreams, what holy aspirations!

At last you wrapped them up again and put them away, wondering how it could have happened. Why the separation, the loneliness, the heartache?

O lonely soul, O aching heart, look up! God knows. God cares. And "no good thing will He withhold from them that walk uprightly." Your part is to live for Him, to put Him first in your life. For if you do, you have His solemn word of promise that nothing really good will be withheld. He has a far better plan for your life than you have. And he wants you to have His best.

Remember this: God is all-wise. Therefore, He *knows* what is best. And then He is all-loving. Hence, He will *do* what is best. Now if He is all-wise and *knows* what is best, and all-loving and will *do* what is best, surely you can trust Him.

No father ever cared more dearly. No husband ever loved more deeply. Not for one moment has He forgotten you. The God who sees the sparrow fall, and who numbers the hairs of your head, has said, "I will never leave thee nor forsake thee," and He never will. He loves you with an everlasting love.

In all points He was tempted as you have been. Hence, He can sympathize. "In all their affliction," the Bible says, "He was afflicted." He knew what it was to be lonely. His disciples all forsook Him and fled. Alone in the garden He prayed. Alone He wept. No one understood Him. All misinterpreted His actions. And when He died, He died alone. Oh, beloved, remember Gethsemane. Remember Calvary. And in your loneliness think of Him.

> *Alone with Thee when others have forsaken*
> *And naught is left save solitude to me;*
> *My weary heart turns, throbbing with emotion,*
> *To find itself at last alone with Thee.*
>
> *Alone, dear Lord, ah yes, alone with Thee!*
> *My aching heart at rest, my spirit free;*
> *My sorrow gone, my burdens all forgotten,*
> *When far away I soar alone with Thee.*

And then, let me remind you of the fact that "all things work together for good to them that love God," for they do. All things. That bitter disappointment, the loss of the one you loved, your bereavement, the vacant chair, the empty cradle, even your misunderstanding, the saddest experience in your life—all things—God will see that they work together for good. He cannot do otherwise. You simply must trust.

Around you is the circle of His will, and nothing can pierce that circle without His permission. Therefore, when it touches you it becomes His will for you. Thus you fit into His plan and He works out His purpose in your life.

Then fear thou not; say always, "It is well!"
If in His will then evil is not ill;
What He ordains is always best for thee,
Ill cannot come unless it be His will.

His love can never fail. Others may change; He never will. He is the "same yesterday, to-day and forever." Human affection is always uncertain. Divine love is unchanging and unchangeable. And oh, how rich, how boundless is God's love! What an ocean of affection is His! And how He longs to lavish it on His children, and so to fill the vacancy and bind up the broken heart. What fathomless love! And it may be yours. Oh, then, accept it. Press up just a little closer. Draw a little nearer. Love Him more. You will soon become conscious of such love and compassion, such mercy and tenderness, such peace and comfort, that you will be more than satisfied. His love will heal your broken heart and close up the wounds. God understands.

God understands your heartache,
He knows the bitter pain;
Oh, trust Him in the darkness,
You cannot trust in vain.

He understands your longing,
Your deepest grief He shares;
Then let Him bear your burden,
He understands, and cares.

So, then, learn to sup with Jesus. Enter into fellowship with Him. Let Him be your Companion, your Friend. Walk with Him, talk with Him. Tell Him all about your aching heart. Unburden your soul. Let Him into the deepest secrets of your life. For there are many things too sacred, too private to tell others. They must forever remain hidden in your breast. But you can trust Him. He will understand at once. So tell Him. And then you will hear His whisper, "Peace, be still," and there will be "a great calm."

"What a Friend we have in Jesus,
All our sins and griefs to bear!
What a privilege to carry
Everything to God in prayer!"

Before long you will realize that you needed these experiences. Needed them to make you tender-hearted and sympathetic. Needed them so that out of your Gethsemane you might be able to comfort others. For you see, beloved, you cannot comfort others until you yourself have been comforted of God. You cannot sympathize with those in sorrow unless you have first suffered yourself. Unless you have been lonely, how are you going to understand the loneliness of others? Unless you have loved and lost, how can you feel for other aching hearts? Only those who have been bereaved can weep with those that weep.

Hence, God had to let you suffer so that you might appreciate the sufferings of others. He knew that he could use you. But first He had to put you in His school of sorrow and train you so that you might know how to sympathize and comfort. And could you have seen the future from the beginning, you would not have rebelled. For you are not the only sufferer in the world; there are thousands everywhere.

Learn, then, to feel for others, and do not be selfish in your grief. Share what God has wrought in you and it will be balm to your own stricken heart. And soon you will thank God for the nights of loneliness and the days of pain. "It was all worthwhile," you will say. "I thank God for every stroke. I can now minister to others." Ah yes, death first, then resurrection, the cross and then the glory. Calvary and then Easter. First the thorns and then the crown. To bless we must bleed.

I, too, have suffered. But in my sorrow I turned to God. Alone I told Him all, cried my heart out, sought Him in the darkness, yielded to His will, and He did not fail me. "Weeping may endure for a night, but joy cometh in the morning," was His first word of promise to me. And presently, one day, alone in the mountains, as the sun was sinking over the distant hills in the west, I heard His voice, and oh, the joy, the peace! It was like the calm after the storm, like sunshine after rain. His song filled my heart. He met me. And that very hour, long, long ago—I can remember it yet—I sat down and wrote, among others, these words:

> *Would I could bring the vision closer, nearer,*
> *And give to you a glimpse of what is mine;*
> *Teach you to know that earth's most cruel affliction*
> *Is not beyond the hand of Love Divine.*

> *And that for each lone life a plan is waiting,*
> *Sketched by the Master Architect above;*
> *Checkered by joy and sorrow, yet proportion'd,*
> *Far more of joy, the proof that God is love.*

Yet sorrow speaks, and in sublime orations,
  Brings to the heart the lessons it would teach;
Sunshine and rain the little seed requiring—
So God ordains to man a part of each.

Darkness and gloom beyond my comprehension
  Until I knelt submissive to His will;
Now all is light, ineffable in brightness—
O wondrous love, beyond my knowledge still.

You see, I said, "Not my will but Thine be done," said it from my heart. And the peace came. Oh no, it is not easy to say, but say it, aching heart, and it will be the sweetest experience you have ever known. "Not my will, not mine, but Thine be done."

And now, in closing, let me suggest something that may help you more than anything I have said.

"Forgetting those things which are behind, and reaching forth unto those things which are before, I press toward the mark for the prize of the high calling of God in Christ Jesus" (Phil. 3: 13, 14).

Beloved, God wants you to forget. Bury the past. Yes, I mean it. Put the letters away. Lay the pictures aside. Keep everything that reminds you of bygone days out of sight. Deliberately turn away and forget. Then face the present and the future anew. Don't allow your thoughts to dwell on the past, but plan and work for the years to come.

Remember, you cannot change what has been. "What I have written, I have written," said Pilate. Ah yes, how true! No anguish of heart, no sad recollections can alter anything! Weep if you will, brood as much as you like, it will make no difference. You will only become the more despondent and melancholy.

Then why despair? Life has not yet ended. Are you

going to be foolish enough to allow the vain regrets of the past to rob you of the joys of the future? If you cannot change it, then why make yourself miserable by dwelling on it? Has the present nothing to offer? Can you not enjoy the future? God tells you to forget. Then do it.

Let me forget the scenes of other days,
  The hallowed dreams that never can come true,
But let me live this day my life anew,
  And for the future build with joy and praise.

Let me forget the visions of the past,
  The wreck of blighted hopes, the years of pain;
Let me forget the pledges made in vain,
  The promises to which I anchored fast.

Consider that life is only just now beginning so far as you are concerned. If you have failed, confess it, and then forever put away the scenes that have haunted your memory for so long. Live for the future. Build your life anew. Let the sad experiences of the past make you just that much stronger for the present. Set life's goal before you and begin again. Achieve once more. If ambition has died, revive it.

Do you remember the vessel that was marred? It was not thrown away. The Bible says, "So he made it again." And so will it be with you. The bird with the broken pinion, by the grace of God, may soar as high again. He can reconstruct and recondition your life. If you will bury your past, both good and bad, lovely and unlovely, successes and failures, if you will turn from the beautiful dreams and the hallowed memories of other days, and set your face towards the future, life will still be worth while. God will not fail you. Soon the gloom will pass away. Hope was never born to die. Trouble cannot always last. Love is bound to triumph yet. God will turn your night to day. Life can never be in vain. Happy days will come again.

And so, dear one, as you turn off my voice and go to your rest, go with a lighter heart, a firmer trust and a brighter hope, and I will be praying for you. Some day, please God, we shall meet, if not here, then up There. And so, until the day break and all the shadows flee away, Good night. God bless you! Good night!

CHAPTER VI

THE GREATEST BOOK IN THE WORLD

I N THE mind free from prejudice and open to facts, there can be no doubt but that the Greatest Book in the World is the Bible.

Its Circulation

In the first place, the Bible is the Greatest Book in the World from a numerical standpoint. Its present circulation exceeds that of any other book. If you visit the leading book stores toward the end of the week, they will name such and such a book as the "best seller." Next week, in all probability, some other will take the lead. But notwithstanding their popularity, the sales of these "best sellers" are daily, weekly and annually surpassed by the sale of the Book of books.

The Bible, in whole or in part, has been translated into more than a thousand different languages and dialects, and of no other book can this be said. It is a remarkable fact that the nearest approach to this is also a religious book. Bunyan's *Pilgrim's Progress* holds a unique place as second to the Bible in this respect.

But the Bible is not a single book; it is a combination of sixty-six books, written by more than thirty-six different writers and covering a period in its composition of 1,600 years.

Its Unity

It was written by men on every plane of social life, from the herdsman and fisherman, up to the king on his throne. It contains history, biography, poetry and law. It begins with the serpent at liberty and ends with the serpent bound. It begins with death, and ends with no more death. It begins with paradise lost and ends with paradise restored.

When the magnificent temple of Solomon was built, the material which was prepared beforehand was brought from all parts of the world. As the people gazed out upon the various quarries that lay so far apart, they would observe nothing but confusion and disorder. But at last all is ready and the great building is slowly erected. Stone fits into stone, rock into rock, until, finally, the beautiful edifice is completed in all its unity. Would the people not realize that behind all there must have been a great architect, a master mind? Most certainly.

And so it was with the Bible. Mere men, living centuries apart, could never write so as to preserve a perfect unity; but back of all, as the centuries rolled away, an unseen Hand was guiding each individual builder. Yes, behind the Bible was the greatest of all architects, the Master of all builders—God. Hence, its unbroken unity.

To illustrate, let us look for a moment at the unity of the four Gospels. These are not four contradictory records of the life of our Lord, but rather four accounts written from different viewpoints. If you wish to secure a perfect representation of a large building, it will be necessary to photograph each of its four sides. And so it is with the four Gospels.

Matthew sees in Jesus the promised Messiah of Israel. He writes for the Jews and aims to convince them that Jesus is the true Messiah. There are more Old Testament quotations in Matthew's Gospel than in any of the others. His is the Gospel of the Kingdom.

Mark sets forth Jesus as the servant, the One who came to serve humanity. "For even the Son of Man came not to be ministered unto but to minister." He is writing for the Romans who knew what it was to have servants and slaves. They were a quick and active people, and so we find him using such words as "forthwith", "straightway", and "immediately", and writing in a short, sharp and decisive manner, in order to arrest their attention.

Luke sees in Jesus the Son of Man, the lowly and humble Nazarene, the Man of many sorrows, who went about doing good. As He entered the homes of the people, sunshine and happiness entered with Him, and when He left, peace and comfort remained behind. Here we have the touching stories of "The Lost Sheep" and "The Prodigal Son," in which all the tenderness and pathos of that great heart of infinite love and compassion manifests itself. His is the Gospel of the poor, and he writes for Gentile converts.

The Gospel of John, unlike the synoptics, gives not so much the externals of Christ's life, but rather the inner and deeper side, the spiritual element. He writes of Jesus as the Son of God. Thus we have His talk with Nicodemus: "Except a man be born again, he cannot see the kingdom of God," and such words as, "whosoever" and "believe", words pertaining to Salvation. And in the last verse of the twentieth chapter his purpose is clearly stated: "But these are written, that ye might believe that Jesus is the Christ, the Son of God; and that believing ye might have life through His name."

John's Gospel was written long after the others. Not until ninety years of his life had passed away did he begin to write, and then out of a full experience he gives us the richest, deepest and best of all.

Its Fascination

Furthermore, the Bible is the Greatest Book in the World because it affords the most fascinating of all study to those who are willing to study it. There is nothing that would bring us more blessing than a study of the Bible. Perhaps the greatest need of the Church to-day is a deeper study of God's Word. In prayer we talk to God, but in Bible study He talks to us, and it is far more important that He talk to us, than it is that we should talk to Him. And so, "As new born babes, desire the sincere milk of the Word, that ye may grow thereby." The men who have accomplished the greatest things for God have all been earnest students of the Bible. A Christian who doesn't know how to use his Bible is like a soldier who doesn't know how to use his weapons.

To a great many the Bible is an uninteresting Book. It might be compared to the stained-glass windows of a church, which in the daytime appear only dull and uninviting. But when the inside is illuminated in the evening, how beautiful the transformation! So when Christ is seen as the Chiefest among ten thousand, shining through the pages of the Bible, it becomes a new Book, a revelation of the Father's love, and a never-ending charm. And we can say with the psalmist of old: "Thy Word is a lamp unto my feet, and a light unto my path."

Its Power

And lastly, the Bible is the Greatest Book in the World because of its transforming and life-giving power. "For the Word of God is quick and powerful, and sharper than any two-edged sword." It has power to lift men. It takes the low and degraded, the immoral and corrupt outcast of society, and makes him a respectable citizen again, clean and pure, a child of God and an heir of Heaven. "Wherewithal shall a young man cleanse his way? by taking heed thereto according to thy Word" (Ps. 119: 9).

It comforts the sad and disheartened. How often, as the shadows are gathering around the weary sufferer and the light is growing dim, has the twenty-third Psalm been requested: "Yea, though I walk through the valley of the shadow of death, I will fear no evil: for Thou art with me; Thy rod and Thy staff they comfort me." Or the fourteenth chapter of John's Gospel: "In my Father's house are many mansions: if it were not so, I would have told you. I go to prepare a place for you. And if I go to prepare a place for you, I will come again, and receive you unto myself; that where I am, there ye may be also." And then, the day breaks, "and the shadows flee away."

Thousands find in it their daily companion and friend. They come to it for comfort when they are sad, for guidance when perplexed. It inspires many of them to deeds of love and sacrifice which make the world richer and better. The poor among them read it and learn to sing songs of joy and gladness in their poverty. The tempted and tried find it a source of new strength and hope.

Bear in mind that there is no situation in life for which you cannot find some word of consolation in the Scripture. If you are afflicted, if you are in adversity or trial, there is a promise for you. In joy or in sorrow, in health or in sickness, in poverty or in riches—in every condition of life God has a promise stored up for you in His Word. In one way or another, every case is met.

Think of it, thousands of exceedingly great and precious promises. To the tired and careworn soul there comes the tender voice of Jesus, saying: "Come unto me all ye that labour and are heavy laden and I will give you rest." To the disheartened and discouraged, "I will never leave thee nor forsake thee." And to the worried and anxious is given the divine assurance, "My God shall supply all your need according to His riches in glory by Christ Jesus."

How many there are, who with the sweet Psalmist of Israel, would exclaim, "O how love I Thy law! it is my meditation all the day." Thousands would suffer any loss, rather than part with the Bible. Hundreds have suffered death itself, rather than bring dishonour upon the Word of the living God.

There is a regrettable tendency today to substitute great writers such as Shakespeare and Tennyson for the Bible. But not until all sorrow has passed away, the tears have ceased to flow, and the Bible has been proved inadequate to meet the needs of man, can we afford to substitute the works of uninspired men. Until that day comes, let us draw our supply from the Word of God, that liveth and abideth forever.

CHAPTER VII

THE HOME OVER THERE

THERE is no sweeter word in the English language than the word "home". The fact that Heaven is pictured to us as a Home endears it to every heart, and brings up a flood of sacred memories and associations.

Possibly there are few songs so deeply loved as "Home, Sweet Home". Yet it is only when far, far away from home and friends in some lonely part of the world that it really grips the heart and brings a great lump to the throat. Is that the way we feel about Heaven? Are we truly pilgrims and strangers here? Oh, then, what a joy to know that when we leave our earthly home we enter our eternal one! There are many here who have no home; there will be none Over There.

But the song that has suggested our theme holds a deeper meaning than even "Home, Sweet Home". Oh, what comfort it imparts, what holy desires are created by it!

> *Oh, think of the Home Over There,*
> *By the side of the river of light,*
> *Where the saints, all immortal and fair,*
> *Are robed in their garments of white.*

Some may wonder why I speak so often about the other life. There are several reasons. I do it because it has so much to do with this one, for it is the great hope of the Home Over There that buoys us up amid all the sorrows and disappointment of earth. It was this hope that enabled the early Martyrs to sing with joy in the midst of the most horrible physical sufferings. They were thinking of the Home Over There.

> *There is joy in the City of God,*
> *And freedom from sorrow and care;*
> *A joy that no tongue can describe,*
> *For Jesus Himself will be there.*

It is the thought of Heaven that keeps our minds off the things of earth. I shall never forget the vision of "Intra Muros". How vividly it portrays the other life, and how quickly earth's treasures lose their charm! Sometimes when the burdens of life are unusually heavy and the vision of the Glory Land is veiled, I can bring it back again by humming over the words of a song I shall never cease to love:

> *One sweetly solemn thought*
> *Comes to me o'er and o'er—*
> *I am nearer Home to-day,*
> *Than ever I've been before.*
>
> *Father, be near when my feet*
> *Are slipping o'er the brink;*
> *For it may be I am nearer Home,*
> *Nearer now than I think.*

When I consider for but one brief moment the wondrous life beyond the grave, and on its untold glories allow my mind to dwell—I marvel that earth's treasures e'er had power to turn my thoughts from Him who gave so much. Then, as the rapture and the splendour of it all breaks in upon my soul, the greatest sacrifice, the hardest lot, or the very best that earth can boast: fame, wealth, power, home, and all else that men count dear—seems to fade away in utter insignificance in the face of countless ages of unbroken peace, rest, union and contentment, the unutterable blessings of God's immeasurable Eternity.

Then, too, there are grey heads among us, men and women who, in a little while, will close their eyes upon the scenes of earth to open them upon the Eternity beyond. And I would comfort these as they await the great change. Their feelings are voiced in the words of that old Scotch hymn sung by a saint of God on the eve of life:

> *I am far frae my hame, an' I'm weary aften-whiles,*
> *For the lang'd for hame bringin' an' my Father's*
> *welcome smiles,*
> *An' I'll ne'er be fu' content until my een do see*
> *The gowden gates o' Heaven, an' my ain countrie.*

But more than that, you and I, my friends, are hastening on to the life beyond the grave, and no one can tell how soon his time will come. Now I would like to know all I can about the world to which I am going. And there is only one place I can go to find out, and that is to the dear old Book. Oh, praise Him for the Bible! For when death robs us of our loved ones it is our only source of information regarding them. Here alone we can find out where they have gone. And these are a few of the things that God tells us in His precious Book await us on the other side:

(1) *Perfect Happiness and Satisfaction*

We live to-day in a world that can never fully satisfy. "Earth is a desert drear, Heaven is my home." The human heart yearns for something else. Listen! "They shall hunger no more, neither thirst any more; neither shall the sun light on them, nor any heat. For the Lamb which is in the midst of the throne shall feed them, and shall lead them unto living fountains of water; and God shall wipe away all tears from their eyes" (Rev. 7: 16, 17).

The things that bring sorrow and pain and unhappiness will be gone forever. Think of it! No tears, no pain, no night, no death, and no separation. A perfect home. "And He shall wipe away every tear from their eyes; and death shall be no more; neither shall there be mourning, nor crying, nor pain any more" (Rev. 21: 4). We are wont to speak of earth as the land of the living. But, oh no! this is the land of the dying. It is in Heaven that there is to be no more death.

Where then are we to seek the satisfaction for which our souls crave? Do earthly possessions bring happiness? Is there anything in this life that can fully meet our need? Dear one, you know there is not. How often have you longed for something more! Even in your moments of greatest rapture has there not come the thought of the change that must sooner or later take place? Earth's joys are fleeting. Nothing here can last. "Change and decay in all around I see." What, then, do we seek? A life that knows no change. A satisfaction that has no end. Happiness, without alloy. Oh, how our hearts crave that fuller life!

(2) *Fuller Knowledge and Comprehension*

The dark things of life will be made plain. The trial, the temptation, the burden, and the sickness, will all be understood Over There. That death—you cannot understand it. How you sat and watched the dear one passing out! How you yearn "for the touch of a vanished hand, and the sound of a voice that is still!" And you wonder why. Why the vacant chair? It seemed so cruel, so unnecessary. But wait. The hidden things are all to be made plain. Knowledge now withheld will then be given, and you will yet rejoice. Take courage, then, sad heart; the night will soon be gone, the day dawn.

> *Not now, but in the coming years,*
> *It may be in the better land,*
> *We'll read the meaning of our tears,*
> *And there, sometime, we'll understand.*

Oh, how we long to know, just to know! Can it be that God would put such cravings in our hearts only to deny us? Surely not. What babes we are! How much we have to learn! God's school awaits us Over Yonder. Our minds, so finite now, yet thirsting still to know, to comprehend, will then leap forth and master knowledge of which we here have never even dreamed.

(3) *Reunion and Recognition*

The rich man recognized both Abraham and Lazarus. Moses and Elijah were easily identified on the Mount. And David, with the utmost confidence in speaking of his dead child, boldly exclaimed: "I shall go to him." Ah yes! there is perfect recognition in the Home Over There.

> *Beautiful faces, radiant with glory,*
> *Waiting and watching, gazing below;*
> *Looking for dear ones, careworn and weary,*
> *Soon to rejoin them, longing to go!*

And you will, ah yes! and know them, every one. Those lips you kissed in death down here will part to speak once more up there. Those eyes that sparkled and laughed while yet on earth will be still more radiant when you meet again. The friends you knew so long ago, the form you used to love, the dear ones old and young—all who knew Him here—you will recognize them, every one, up there. "We shall know as we are known." Forget them not, beloved, for they are yours forever.

(4) *Unhindered Growth and Progress*

We will begin exactly where we left off. If we have reached the third step here it will be from that point we shall start up there. The more we advance in spirituality here, the less we have to make up Over There. Oh, that this thought might act as an incentive to spur us on till we are so transformed, so mature that our starting point up yonder may be the highest possible.

How glorious to be always ready! What if death should find us unprepared! Thank God, we can live here so close to Him, so completely in the centre of His will, so well-pleasing in His sight, that it will seem most natural to step from this sphere to the next, there to continue our spiritual and mental development. Growth will not cease with death, nor progress end. "Still there's more to follow."

(5) *Ceaseless Activity and Work*

"And they serve Him day and night in His temple" (Rev. 7: 15). Angels to be judged. It may be worlds to be ruled. And God wants strong characters for His mighty tasks both here and there. Perhaps that is why great souls are often taken in early life just at their best. He needs them. We are all building character. Every thought, word, and deed makes its contribution. Is it a great character we are building? Can He use us up there?

But what a joy it is to work! How weary we grow of doing nothing! And we love our work; for is it not our very meat and drink? God help the man who has no work, nothing to occupy his time! But how tired we get! These physical bodies of ours—how little they can stand! If only we could labour on and on and on! "I am tired in the work," we say, "but not of it." Thank God, there is a life beyond the grave where we can never more be tired. It matters not what may be the task, nor how many centuries it may take to accomplish it, we will be able to work on and on and on, craving neither rest nor relaxation, never, never weary again. Dear Lord, what a prospect!

> 'Tis when I think of all that Heaven holds,
> The wondrous joy that God to man unfolds,
> The life of perfect bliss apart from pain,
> The land where death and sickness never reign,
>
> The home of many mansions bright and fair,
> The life that feels no sorrow, knows no care;
> Where tears are wiped from ev'ry weeping eye,
> Where immortality shall never die;
>
> And where the sun's hot rays shall shine no more,
> The blast of winter be forever o'er;
> Our dearest friends shall never from us part,
> And love alone shall rule in ev'ry heart;
>
> We nevermore shall know a lonely night,
> For night shall pass away 'mid Heaven's light;
> The tired, the weary, wayworn feet shall rest,
> The lame, the halt, shall be forever blest,

The blind shall once again receive their sight,
And all the wrongs of earth shall be made right;
There with our Saviour we shall ever be
Throughout the ages of Eternity;

And when we've been with Him a million years
No more to dwell amid this vale of tears,
We'll have, O wondrous thought! no less to live,
For Everlasting Life is His to give—

'Tis when on scenes like this I dwell in thought
And know that I am saved, but some are not,
With pleading voice and yearning heart I go
That Jesus Christ the world may come to know,

That through His wondrous death upon the cross
They might not suffer such tremendous loss,
But share in all that Heaven holds for me,
And dwell with Him throughout Eternity.

And so, my friends, I would urge you to think of Heaven. But I would remind you that Heaven is a prepared place for a prepared people, and that the preparation must begin here. We prepare for everything else, journeys, homes, etc., but do we prepare for Heaven? For unless our likes and dislikes are according to those of the people with whom we dwell we cannot be happy. If we were to reach Heaven unsaved our first plea would be, "Oh, let me get out of here!" A sinner in the company of Christians is the most miserable person imaginable.

My friend, are you ready for the great change? Does the thought of the Home Over There thrill your heart with joy? Have you a desire to depart and be with Christ? Can you afford to miss such happiness? Are you one of

His? If not, I beg of you this moment to receive Jesus Christ as your own personal Saviour, for apart from Him there can be no Heaven. He is the only Way to the Home Over There.

There's a Home beyond the shadows far away from sin
*   and pain,*
*   Where the sorrows of the world will be no more;*
There are many, many mansions for the weary, worn
*   and sad,*
*   Where the strife and toil of earth will all be o' er.*

CHAPTER VIII

VIRGIL'S ESCAPE

IT WAS night. Heavy, black clouds massed themselves against the sky, and hung low over the waves. The sea, lashed to fury by the wild wind, foamed and raged among the rocks along the battlements of the darkened heavens, while ever and anon the awful scene was revealed for a moment by a flash of lightning, followed by blackness that could almost be felt. Trees tore at their roots as the hurricane bent them this way and that.

It was night. Virgil stirred restlessly, as his wife bent over his emaciated form. Startled by the blinding flashes of lightning and trembling from head to foot with each peal of thunder, he grabbed at the sides of the bed, or attempted to spring up, his eyes staring wildly about the room. Great drops of sweat stood out on his brow. His voice was hoarse. He breathed in quick, sharp jerks.

Suddenly he sat upright, his eyes almost starting from their sockets.

"Wife, look! look there!" he cried, throwing his arms up as if in an effort to ward off an attack.

"What is it, Virgil? I see nothing," responded the woman, though startled by the wild expression in her husband's eyes.

"Nothing! Why, look at them! They are as plain as you are, and they watch me, they wait for me. Wife! Wife, for God's sake—!" And the dying man flung his face in his pillow to shut out the dreaded sight.

"Come, Virgil, it is only your imagination, quickened by the awful storm that is raging," said his wife, with a note of assurance in her voice.

Slowly, fearfully, gripping the sides of the bed with both hands, he turned his head and eyes once again towards the dreaded corner. But it was only for a second for, with the expression of a doomed soul, he shrieked in anguish, and grabbing his hair between his fingers, tore it out by the roots, then fell back exhausted, his eyes still riveted on the apparition in the corner.

"Wife," he began, after remaining thus for full five minutes, "wife, there are five of them. They stand in a group together in that corner," indicating the corner by a nod of his head; "and they have the appearance of the spirits of damned souls. See, they are waiting, waiting for me, and soon, soon I, too, shall be with them. Great God, my soul is damned, damned, damned."

Virgil fell back. The thunders crashed as though to add emphasis to what he had just said. A sudden flash of lightning illuminated the darkened room, and for one brief moment lit up the face of the wretched man. It was convulsed with agony; the eyes, wide open, seemed ready to burst out of their sockets, which caused his wife to spring to her feet in terror and rush down to the room below, while the wind blew in maddened blasts against the lonely house.

Virgil knew he was dead, that is, as men speak of death, for in a moment he was standing beside the bed, looking down at the body in which he had lived and moved and had his being for some thirty years. But he was immediately conscious of a great danger and, with the swiftness of lightning, he sped to the farther side of the room.

"Now we can take him," uttered a voice that seemed close by his side.

Looking up, he saw clearly the five spirits that he had seen before, coming towards him, while a wild, nameless fear clutched at his heart. With lightning-like speed he darted hither and thither, seeking to evade his pursuers, but in vain. He was surrounded in a moment, and escape, he knew, was impossible.

"What do you want with me?" he cried, suddenly turning and, with his back against the wall, standing at bay.

"You must come with us now," answered the spirit nearest him. "You know you are our property. Be quick! We have waited long enough already. Let us hurry. He will be expecting us soon." And they closed in upon him.

"He will be waiting! Who? Where are we going?" cried Virgil, speeding out of their grasp.

"You will soon know all," replied another. "It is useless to resist. You can't get away. Everyone must go to his own place."

But Virgil was not ready to yield so easily, though he felt all the time that escape was impossible, and that it was useless to resist.

Hither and thither he darted, the five of them pursuing him. First up and then down, around and around the room, behind this piece of furniture and that. Finally, in sheer desperation, he dashed himself, as he thought, against the wall, and found to his amazement that he was able to pass through it as though it did not exist. Then he remembered that he was no longer in a body subject to natural law. Casting one last hasty glance at his own corpse stretched on the bed, he sped out into the blackness of darkness and into the night.

The storm had no terror for him now. The huge waves still broke upon the rocks in surging foam. The lightning flashed as before and the thunder roared, even louder and more frequently, while the wind blew a hurricane. But these were now his friends, and to lose himself in them and thus elude his horrible pursuers was his one and only thought.

But it was not to be. On they came with lightning-like speed. The struggle for liberty was of short duration. Together they pounced upon him, and held him captive. He stopped struggling, knowing that it was useless. In a moment they were out of the storm, and far down in the heart of the earth. All was silence now, except for the noise made by their own swift passage.

"Where are we going?" cried the wretched prisoner, as they dragged him down.

"To Hades," answered one of his captors, without a moment's pause.

Oh, the agony of that thought! How memory rose up and lashed him! What opportunities he had missed! How often he had ignored the invitation. And now, now at last he was being taken to the abode of the damned—he, Virgil the moralist, who would not humble himself and accept the Christ. A thousand scenes flashed before him during those awful moments, scenes that brought nothing but torment to his already tormented brain, and as though compelled by an invisible power, he repeated some verses that he had read only two weeks before:

> *Lost, lost, lost! No God, no hope, no light,*
> *Bound for a land of death and endless night;*
> *Lost to the Christ who gave His life for thee,*
> *Doomed to a world of woe and misery!*

"Ah, yes, that's it. I boasted of my moral and religious life. No one lived better. Few were more faithful to their church. Highly respected, and praised for my philanthropic enterprises, I rested in my own righteousness, not realizing that God looked upon my beautiful, self-made

E

character as 'filthy rags'. Nor would I take the place of a sinner and trust alone in the merits of the shed blood of Calvary's cross. God's Son had no place in my life. Oh, for another opportunity! But, it is too late, too late, too late!" he wailed as he sped on.

Down, down, down! Would it never end? Of course, it took but a few moments, yet to Virgil it seemed hours. Down, down, down! If so much could pass through his brain in a few seconds, however would he endure the tormenting thoughts of an endless eternity! Down, down, down! It seemed that he could already hear the groans and cries from the infernal pit.

Suddenly, with a shriek of despair he began to struggle once more. With frantic efforts, he sought to free himself. At times he thought he felt the grasp of his captors loosening. Somehow, the descent grew less rapid. He became less and less conscious of his surroundings. Presently, in his bewilderment, he heard again the crash of thunder and the roaring of the waves. A moment later he was startled by a blinding flash of lightning.

Opening his eyes, he was amazed to see his wife bending over him, as he lay on the bed, and the old familiar objects of furniture faintly outlined by the dim light.

"There, Virgil," she was saying, "you are better now. The crisis is past. I thought you were gone, but you have rallied at last, and you will soon be well again," she continued in an assuring tone.

"Thank God! Thank God!" was all he could murmur, as he began to realize that he was still alive, while a flood of grateful tears suffused his cheeks.

Closing his eyes, he remained for some time in prayer. His wife thought he had dozed off, and was congratulating herself, but presently he again opened them, while a bright light overspread all his features, and a look of inexpressible peace and joy beamed on his countenance.

"Wife," he said, "read me those words that you read a week ago, the ones about which I insisted there was too much certainty and assurance."

Picking up a hymn-book that lay nearby, too amazed to question him, she hastily turned over a few pages and began:

> *Saved! saved! saved! my sins are all forgiv'n;*
> *Christ is mine; I'm on my way to Heav'n;*
> *Once a guilty sinner, lost, undone,*
> *Now a child of God, saved through His Son.*

Virgil slept. Rest, the first real rest that he ever knew, was depicted on his features. He had no fear.

A week passed. Slowly but surely he grew weaker and weaker. Another and more serious crisis was rapidly approaching. At the end of seven days it came.

It was night. A second storm, fully as bad, if not worse than the first, broke upon the lonely coast. Mighty peals of thunder again shook the earth. Lightning flashed once more. The billows, piled mountain high, hurled themselves against the angry rocks.

Suddenly, the sick man, as though sustained by a supernatural power, raised himself on his elbow, and, pointing eagerly to the memorable corner of the dismally lighted room, exclaimed:

"Look, wife, look! Two. But, oh, what faces! How beautiful!" And a radiant smile broke over his countenance, while a light of welcome sprang from his eyes.

"Why, Virgil," questioned the woman, "what is it? Are they like the five you saw before?"

"Oh, no, no, wife! I'm not afraid of these. Oh, how glorious they are! And they have come for me. They are waiting, waiting, even now. Oh how glad I am to go!"

Exhausted he lay back, his eyes still riveted on the figures in the corner.

"Are they still there?" inquired his wife, a little later.

"Oh, yes; and they are so real, more real than you are. Can't you see them? Look, they are coming towards me now. Oh, welcome! welcome! angels of God!" And he held out his arms in eager anticipation, while a light that never shone on land or sea beamed from his eyes.

"The angel of the Lord encampeth round about them that fear Him, and delivereth them," murmured his wife, as she hovered over him.

Still the thunder roared and the lightning flashed. Still the angry waves broke in billows of foam on the lonely coast. And still the wind tore around the rickety old house and howled among the trees.

But Virgil heard it not. For him the storm could hold no terrors. Another journey had been taken, and this time he was glad to go. He was now in different company, and his destination led up—not down. Oh, what a glorious escape!

CHAPTER IX

THE GREATEST STORY EVER TOLD!

MANY years ago an African chief visited Queen Victoria in England. When he was leaving he asked her a question. "Your Majesty," he inquired, "what is the secret of England's greatness?" "The Bible," was the immediate response of the Queen.

The Bible is the greatest Book in the world. No man is educated until he knows it. I have read it every day of my life for over fifty years, and I am going to read it every day until I see my Saviour face to face. I would urge you to do the same.

This Book means more to me than any other book. It is my meat and my drink. The more I study it, the more I love it. There is no other like it. It is God's Book. When I read it God speaks to me. I hear His voice. By it men are saved. By it men live. And by it men are going to be judged. It is our one and only authority. This Book will keep you from sin, or sin will keep you from this Book.

Now the greatest book in the Bible is the Gospel of John. And the greatest chapter in John's Gospel is the third. The greatest verse in the third chapter is the sixteenth. And this is what it says: "For God so loved the world, that He gave His only begotten Son, that whosoever believeth in Him should not perish, but have everlasting life." That is the greatest story ever told.

This, my friends, is the heart of the Gospel. More souls have been saved through John 3: 16 than through any other verse. It is the best-known verse in the Bible and it has been translated into more languages than any other. It is the greatest statement concerning the love of God on record. Moreover it is God's Word.

About a thousand years ago now, a Jewish song-writer, Meir Ben-Isaac Nehoric, wrote a stanza about the love of God, which was later published in *A Book of Jewish Thoughts*, compiled by Joseph Herman Hertz, Chief Rabbi of the British Empire. But no one ever heard of it until one day it was found pencilled on the wall of an insane asylum by an inmate who had died. How he had found it no one will ever know. In my mind it is the greatest poem on the love of God ever written. Here it is:

> *Could we with ink the ocean fill,*
> *And were the skies of parchment made;*
> *Were ev'ry stalk on earth a quill,*
> *And ev'ry man a scribe by trade;*
> *To write the love of God above*
> *Would drain the ocean dry;*
> *Nor could the scroll contain the whole,*
> *Though stretched from sky to sky.*

In John 3: 16, we have four tremendous statements regarding the love of God.

First—"For God so Loved the World"

"For *God* so loved . . ." Salvation starts with God. You had nothing to do with it. Before you were born God provided it for you. Don't think you can discover God. You never can. God is revealed, not discovered. He took the first step.

"For God *so* loved . . ." That little word "so" speaks volumes. It explains all that follows, all that Christ endured for you, all that God suffered when He gave Christ. All He saves you from and all that He provides for you is because He *so* loved you.

"For God so *loved* . . ." The gods of the heathen are gods of hate and fear. Our God is a God of love. The heathen are afraid of their gods. We love our God. Their gods are gods of judgment, power and cruelty bent on doing them injury. Our God is a God of judgment and power also, but first and foremost He is a God of love, seeking to do us good.

God does not love man's sin, but He loves man. You do not love your child's disease but you love your child. Such love as God's is unfathomable. It is a love that cannot be understood, but a love that is real nevertheless. I want you, my friend, to know that God loves you. He loves you no matter what you have done, no matter how great your sin, and He always will love you in spite of your attitude towards Him.

"For God so loved the *World* . . ." That is what makes it impossible for the human mind to comprehend the love of God. The world is made up of rebels, men who have turned their backs on God. Yet, in spite of their rebellion God loved them. The Bible says that "God commendeth His love towards us in that while we were yet sinners, Christ died for us" (Rom. 5: 8); and again it says "Christ died for the ungodly" (Rom. 5: 6). God loved not alone the good but the bad. When Jesus was being nailed to the cross, He prayed, "Father, forgive them; for they know not what they do" (Luke 23: 34). Such love is not human; it is divine. In spite of your enmity, God loves you. What marvellous, matchless love!

Had God wiped out the race as He destroyed the Antediluvians by the flood, and Sodom and Gomorrah by fire, we could have understood it, for that is what man would have done. We did not forgive the Nazi leaders of Germany and give them another chance; we executed them. The Communists of China and Korea cruelly tortured their victims in a most revolting manner. Such is man's inhumanity to man. That is the way man acts. But not so God. His love forgives. God is merciful. He loves the unlovely, the rebellious and the sinful. Such love is super-natural. Only God loves like that.

Had He loved only the lovely the good and obedient, we could have understood it, for we love those who love us. We love our friends; that is human love. But God loves His enemies. He loves the disobedient and sinful. That love we cannot understand. It is beyond our comprehension.

The prodigal's father, you remember, loved his erring son, even though he disgraced him by his life of debauchery and sin. He was waiting with outstretched arms to receive him. "This my son was dead and is alive again," he cried. "He was lost, and is found" (Luke 15: 24). What a welcome! Such is the love of God.

Second—"That He Gave His Only Begotten Son"

"For God so loved the world that He *gave* . . ." Love demands sacrifice. Love produces action. Love must demonstrate itself. That is true even of human love. God has proved His love by giving.

"For God so loved the world that He gave His only begotten *Son* . . ." He could have sent an angel or even an archangel, but He didn't. He sent His Son, His nearest and His dearest. Nothing could have demonstrated His love like the giving of His only begotten Son. A father will give everything he possesses before he will give his son.

Bear in mind, if you will, that God could have rescued His Son even from the cross, and yet He let Him suffer and never raised a hand to save Him. Would you have done that? Could you, as a father, have let your son suffer such excruciating agony, knowing full well that you had the power to rescue him, to save him from it all, and yet never make an effort to do anything? Impossible! There isn't a father in the world who could stand by and see wicked men drive cruel spikes into the hands and feet of his son and not make an effort to save him.

But God did. God allowed His Son to die when He could have rescued Him. That is what makes His love so wonderful. It is a love beyond human understanding. It is not human; it is divine. God's love is so great that He could allow His son to suffer and die and make no effort to save Him, when He could have done so at any time. Such love, I say, is beyond human comprehension. He did it because of His love for you. To save you He had to let His Son die.

Isaac, you remember, was saved, for just as Abraham was about to slay him God cried out, "Abraham, Abraham, lay not thine hand upon the lad" (Gen. 22: 12). But when Jesus, in the agony of His soul, exclaimed, "My God, my God, why hast Thou forsaken me?" (Matt. 27: 46), there was no voice that answered. God turned away His face and let Him die. To save you He had to sacrifice His Son. Oh, what love!

Third—"That Whosoever Believeth in Him"

Now there are three great things in this statement expressed by three words.

First, *whosoever*. Here we have the universality of God's offer of salvation. It is for you, for me, or for anybody else. It takes in the yellow and the brown, the black and the white. It includes sinners of the deepest dye, as well as those who have lived moral and upright lives. It makes no difference what a man is or what he has done, he is included in God's *whosoever*.

Peter thought it was only for the Jews, and God had to give him a special vision before he would go to the Gentiles. God's love is universal, and so is His salvation. It is for Jew and Gentile alike.

I urge you then, to come to Him. You need not fear, no matter what you have done or who you are. God offers you salvation just like anybody else. Drunkards, adulterers, murderers, harlots, liars, thieves, dope-fiends, blasphemers—all may come. God says, *whosoever*.

The second word is the word *believeth*. "Whosoever *believeth* in Him." Faith connects the sinner with God. It simply means trusting Jesus Christ. In other words, you must lean your whole weight on Him. It is a word of action. It has nothing whatever to do with your intellect. It does not say that you must believe certain things about Jesus Christ; it says you must receive Him. "Put your trust in the Lord Jesus, and you will be saved."

You must trust Him as you trust an elevator when you step into it; as you trust a boat when you go aboard; as you trust a train when you enter it. Forget your intellect. Never mind what you believe or what you do not believe. Dare to venture all on Jesus Christ; that is trust. You have believed all your life, now you must act, and when you do you will be saved.

It is "not of works" (Eph. 2: 9). There is nothing you can do to merit it. All your prayers and fastings will not save you. All your churchgoing and religious practices will be unavailing. Penance, self-denial, bodily afflictions, pilgrimages—works of any kind—all, yea, all, will be ineffective. For you are saved, not by works, but by faith.

The third word is the word *Him,* referring, of course, to the Lord Jesus Christ. "Whosoever believeth in Him." Do not worry about your faith. It makes no difference whether you have much or little, nor what kind of faith it is. It may only be like a grain of mustard seed. Forget your faith. Think now of the Object of your faith. Think of the One you are to trust. Put your faith in a person and let that person be the Lord Jesus Christ. It is not your *faith* that saves you; it is Christ.

If you put your faith in the wrong person you will never be saved. If you put your faith in religion or in the church you will not be saved. If you put it in your good works, your morality, again, you will not be saved; but if you put it in Christ He will save you. "Put your trust in the Lord Jesus, and you will be saved" (Acts 16: 31, N.E.B.).

Fourth—"Should not Perish but have Everlasting Life"

There are two things here. First, we are saved from something—"should not perish". We are saved from death. Second, we are given something—"but have everlasting life". We are given Life.

To perish means to die, and to die eternally means to be forever separated from God. That is spiritual death. According to God's word, men are "dead in trespasses and in sins" (Eph. 2: 1), and they have to be quickened into life. Jesus says, "Ye shall die in your sins" (John 8: 24). In other words, unless you receive eternal life you will pass out of this life as you are, namely, "dead in trespasses and in sins".

Look at this fruit. See these vegetables. They all look good. But they are perishing. They are in a state of death. Soon they will become corrupt. Little by little they will rot away. As a matter of fact, they are dead already, for they have been severed from the tree and from the vine. So it is with you. Appearances do not matter. You are already dead; you are right now perishing. Eternal death will be your doom. There is no hope; you cannot be saved—unless you are quickened into life, unless you are grafted into God.

Now God wants to save you from death, and so He offers you life, everlasting life. And I come to you today as His ambassador, with His message of life, eternal life. I offer you now God-life, uncreated life, the life of the ages. Will you have it? Do you want to remain in a state of death? Or do you want this glorious, indestructible Life that God now offers you? It is for you to decide.

I cannot explain it. I do not understand it myself, but I know I have it. I have had it since I accepted Jesus Christ as my Saviour. I became a partaker of divine life and that life is mine today. I know where I am going. Death will not mean a plunge into the dark so far as I am concerned. He "loved me, and gave Himself for me" (Gal. 2: 20). I accepted Him as my Saviour and now I have His life. Therefore, I will never perish, and no one will ever pluck me out of His hand. I am His and He is mine, and mine for all eternity.

This, my friend, is the love of God. Is it not wonderful? What matchless grace! What a glorious revelation! How can you spurn it? How can you turn away? What will you say when you stand before Him? He can forgive anything. But to despise His love, to spurn His offer of mercy, to reject His only begotten Son—that is something that never can be forgiven.

I plead with you because God loves you. This one verse alone is sufficient to prove it. Herein is the Gospel. It is now for you to open your heart and receive the Lord Jesus Christ as your own personal Saviour. "For God so loved the world, that He gave His only begotten son, that whosoever believeth in Him should not perish, but have everlasting life.

"Can You Tell Me the Way to Heaven?"

Let me tell you a story. I read it in a tract. It is rather long, so I am going to condense it for you.

It was during the First World War. Shells were bursting all around. Presently there was a black cloud as pieces of shrapnel came whizzing past. Poor Bert fell like a log. Tiny Tim (6 ft. 3 ins.) jumped down beside him and then returned to his place in the trench.

Suddenly there was a startled cry, "Can you tell me the way to Heaven?" Tiny jumped down again. "The way to Heaven? I'm sorry, chum, I don't know the way, but I'll ask the other fellows."

He returned to the fire-step and walked along to the next man and asked him, but he did not know. So he went on to the man beyond him, but he did not know either. Jumping down, he walked around the trench into the next fire-bay, jumped up on the fire-step and inquired of the third man. Then he went from one to another until he had asked seven men the same question, but none of them knew the way to Heaven.

Leaving that part of the trench, he went on to the next. His question was always the same, "Bert is dying. He wants to know the way to Heaven. Can you tell him the way?" He had now asked sixteen men, but not one of them could answer his question.

Finally Tiny Tim reached a machine-gunner sitting alone with his gun, his eyes glued on the German lines. The gunner felt a thump on his back and then heard a voice shouting, "Gunner, there is a chap in our company who has been hit. He's dying and he wants to know the way to Heaven. Can you tell him the way?"

The machine-gunner turned around and a smile lit up his face as he replied. "Yes," he said, "I know the way, but I cannot get along the trench. I dare not leave my gun. But wait." Thrusting his hand into his pocket he pulled out a little Testament. Quickly turning over the pages, he said, "Look here, chum, this is the way to Heaven, that verse there, John 3: 16. I'll turn the leaves back, you put your thumb on that verse, and tell him that is the way to Heaven."

Quickly Tiny Tim rushed back. He jumped down beside Bert, who lay so still that for a moment he thought he had gone. He touched his shoulder. "I've got it, Bert," he exclaimed. "Here it is, the way to Heaven, John 3: 16, 'For God so loved the world, that He gave His only begotten Son, that whosoever believeth in Him should not perish, but have everlasting life'."

Poor Bert's eyes were wide open now. He was drinking in every word. What a scene it was—Tiny Tim kneeling on the bottom of the trench, his great hand holding the little Testament, the tears running down his cheeks reading again and again those life-giving words in the ears of Bert.

A look of peace came over the face of the dying man as he kept gasping out "whosoever". After a bit he lay quiet and still again. Tiny Tim got back on the firing step. All at once he called out, "Look, chaps!" And there was Bert. With one last great effort he raised himself up. He seemed to be gazing at the little piece of blue sky just visible from the trench. His hands were stretched toward it. His face lit up with angelic glory, and with one last gasp, "whosoever", he fell back dead.

Yes, Bert had found the way to Heaven. What a change! One moment in a trench on the battlefield, the next with Christ. What about you? Have you, too, found the way? If not, read the verse again. It is the greatest

verse in the Bible. Then open your heart to the Lord
Jesus Christ and accept Him as your own personal
Saviour. Will you do it? Do it and do it—NOW.

"For God so loved the world, that He gave His only
begotten Son, that whosoever believeth in Him should not
perish, but have everlasting life." That, my friends, is the
greatest story ever told.

CHAPTER X

THE MAN WHO PRAYED TO A SAINT

DID you ever hear the story of Saint Abraham? It is a weird story and yet it is true. It is the story of two pictures, one—this side the grave, the other —the other side. The pictures are of two men, the first in this world, the second in the next.

The First Picture

In the first picture there is a rich man—a man of the world. He was prosperous and contented. He had all that money could buy. He lived in a mansion, had servants to wait on him, and fared sumptuously every day. Depressions never affected him, for he had abundance.

I have no doubt but that he was highly respected in his community. He had many friends. Rich men generally do. His clothing was of the best, purple and fine linen. He must have held an important position. In any case, he lived in luxury and wanted for nothing.

God did not condemn him for being rich, that is, if he got his riches honestly. He must have been thrifty and industrious. Those who are lazy do not make money. He had used his brains. He had saved. He was not a spend-thrift. And he did not idle away his time, taking it for granted that the country owed him a living. He had invested his talents to the best of his ability and had prospered. The Jews, you know, always considered it a sign of God's favour when a man made good. No, there is not a word of censure because he was rich.

The trouble was, as with so many, both rich and poor, he had left God out of his life. He did not feel his need of God. He lived for himself and for himself alone. And he had a heart of stone, for he was unmoved by the sight of poverty right at his door. He showed no mercy. All that he got he kept. He had nothing for others, nothing for God's work. Self-satisfied as he was, he did not take God into account. I have known rich men who have been humble, devoted followers of the Lord Jesus Christ, who have used their money for God's glory and have been a blessing to thousands. But this man had no use for God. God was not in his thoughts.

Now there is another part to this first picture. It portrays a beggar by the name of Lazarus. Day after day he crawls to the estate of the rich man and, unable to stand, lies at his door, hoping for some of the crumbs so eagerly devoured by the hungry dogs under the table. But generally the dogs get there first and the beggar is denied.

Lazarus, almost devoid of clothing, is covered with sores, ugly running sores, all too common in the East. No physician is sent by the rich man to take care of him. No comfortable bed is provided upon which he can rest his weary body. No food is given to him. In fact, he seems to be without friends. But no, he is not alone; the dogs are his companions, for they, too, are hungry and they seem to be able to sympathize with him. At any rate they gather around and lick his sores. Poor Lazarus! What a tragedy!

Death

And so they live, the rich man and the beggar. But at last, as with all mankind, life ends and death comes. Both die, first the beggar and then the rich man.

One day the servants notice that the dogs are acting strangely. Some of them look as though they have been gnawing on human flesh. They look—and, behold, the emaciated body of the beggar, or what is left of it. Some-one dumps it in a ditch, out of sight, and Lazarus is no more. Never again will the rich man be plagued with his presence. Never again will the dogs lick his sores. He is gone and gone forever, or so the rich man thinks, if in-deed he thinks at all. "And a good riddance, too," he ejaculates, as he makes his way in his purple and fine linen to his heavily laden table, while his servants hurry to wait on him. Poor Lazarus! No longer will he suffer with the cold. Never again will he feel the pangs of hunger. No more will his sores itch and burn. His poor, nude body, racked by pain, foul and unkempt, is at last stiff and lifeless.

But now it is the rich man's turn, for he, too, must die. He sends for the best physicians, for he is deathly sick. Medicines are prescribed. Every remedy known to medical skill is used. Servants tiptoe back and forth. There upon his luxurious bed he lies breathing heavily. No effort is spared to save his life. In the grate a fire is burning to keep him warm. Friends and relatives gather round. But it is all of no use. Money cannot save him. The rich man, too, dies.

Lavish are the preparations made for his funeral. It must be one of the best, in keeping with his station in life. No modest Christian funeral for him. The city's most famous undertaker is there. The most expensive mourners are engaged. No such coffin was ever seen before, at least not in his community. It is the best that money can buy. The pall-bearers are his richest and closest associates. They carry it on their shoulders. He is lauded by every-one. And he is buried in his own sepulchre, in the most prominent part of the cemetery—a sepulchre fit for a

king. It is a grand spectacle and for days the funeral of
the rich man is the talk of the town. "He was buried."
Yes, he was buried, while the beggar was not. And that
is the end.

The Second Picture

The *END* did I say? Has the story indeed closed? Is
there nothing more? What, death the end? NEVER!
It would have been had it not been for Jesus. But Jesus
saw what transpired immediately after. He could see into
the other life. He knew what had happened. He might
have ended the story where we would have had to end it,
but he didn't. He saw beyond. And Jesus draws back
the veil, and now He goes on with the story of the rich
man and the beggar. There is another picture. It is a
picture of life beyond the grave. Let us look at it.

First of all, Jesus directs our attention to the beggar. He
sees him die. So do we. But He sees what happens the
moment he leaves his body. We cannot, so He tells us.
Jesus sees the angels of God. They are standing near by,
invisible to mortal eyes, invisible as yet, to the beggar
himself. They wait for him to draw his last breath and
to vacate his tenement of clay.

At last it is all over, his struggles cease, and in a moment
he is slipping from his fleshly imprisonment. A moment
later and he is free. He looks around. The scenery has not
changed. There is the mansion of the rich man. There are
the dogs. And there beside him is the body that was once
his. Suddenly he glances up, and there, to his amazement,
are the angels, and with a glad smile he turns toward them.
Eagerly they encircle him. Comforting words are spoken.
They bear him aloft. He is conducted to Abraham's
bosom, the Paradise of God. Oh, what a scene! What a
glorious experience!

My friend, let me pause a moment. Why do you fear

death? Do you not know Jesus, and is He not your Saviour? Then let me say that you have no need to fear. You will not be alone. Even now the angels are waiting for you. The moment you close your eyes on this life they will be there to welcome you. You cannot see them, but you will see them then. They will show you the way. You wouldn't know it yourself, but they will guide you. They will bear you Home.

But what of the rich man? We left him in a rich man's sepulchre. Now we see him again, as Jesus continues the story. And where is he? In Hades, the prison house of hell-bound souls. What is his condition? He is in "torments". And as he suffers, he looks up and sees the beggar, Lazarus, afar off, in Abraham's bosom. What a contrast! Yes, and what a calamity!

He is quite conscious, you see. There is no indication of soul-sleep, nor has he been annihilated. He is there, and he is conscious of all that is going on around him. He sees, he hears, he speaks, he feels, he suffers. The unconscious do not see or hear, neither do they speak, feel and suffer. He is not unconscious.

Prayer in Hades

Now at last the rich man prays. I say at last, for I doubt if he had ever prayed before. As a matter of fact, he never before felt the need of prayer. He had all he required and did not have to ask for anything. At least, he thought he had, but he was not conscious of his greatest need, his need of God.

And so now he prays. Why not? There is nothing wrong with praying, is there? We all need prayer. Prayer is all right. It is a good thing to pray. But the rich man's praying got him nowhere. What was the matter? Two things.

First, he prayed to the wrong person. He prayed to a saint. "Father Abraham," he cried. Now Abraham was one of the greatest of all the saints. And if Saint Abraham couldn't help him, then what saint could? Why people should pray to a lesser saint when the greatest can do nothing for them, I cannot understand. And yet they do. They pray to all the little saints—Saint Nicholas, Saint Christopher, Saint Joseph, Saint Anthony, Saint Terassah, and, of course, the Virgin Mary. But who are they in comparison to Saint Abraham? If one of the greatest of all the saints cannot help, of what use is it to pray to the lesser saints? Surely if any saint could answer prayer Saint Abraham could. But not a thing could he do. So it is of no use praying to a saint. "There is one God, and one Mediator between God and men, the man Christ Jesus" (1 Tim. 2: 5), and he should have prayed to Him. But he prayed to the wrong person. That was his first mistake.

Second, he prayed too late. He should have prayed while he was still in the body. He should have prayed on earth. But he waited until he had departed from this life and now it is too late. Prayer is never answered in Hell. Hades is not a place to pray. And millions are making the same mistake today. They will not take time to pray now, but they will pray in the midst of their misery hereafter, and then it will be too late. They will cry, but their cry will be in vain. Their wails will go unheeded there. Now is the time to pray. The rich man prayed too late. That was his second mistake.

His First Petition

In his prayer he offered three petitions, and I want you to note, if you will, how they were dealt with. Here, then, is the first:

"Father Abraham, have mercy on me, and send Lazarus, that he may dip the tip of his finger in water, and cool my tongue; for I am tormented in this flame."

It was a prayer for himself. It was a cry for mercy. "Water! Water!" Not a pailful. Not a cupful. Not even a spoonful. Just a drop. A dip of his finger, not even the hand. And not even the whole finger—just the tip of it. Oh, what desperation! What torture and misery! No water in Hell? No, not a drop. Only devouring flames. Unspeakable torment.

I say it was a prayer for mercy. Yes, but he had showed no mercy when he had the opportunity. Not even to Lazarus. His heart was as hard as flint. He knew not the meaning of the word. And now he cries for mercy.

And Lazarus, the beggar—Lazarus who had been beneath his notice on earth—Lazarus whose services he never needed before, Lazarus is now his one and only hope. "Send Lazarus." He was now, he thought, his only friend. Oh, if only Lazarus could help him! And in a wail of agony he offers his petition.

But now for Abraham's reply. Let me quote it for you in his own words.

"Son, remember that thou in thy lifetime receivedst thy good things, and likewise Lazarus evil things: but now he is comforted, and thou art tormented."

"Son, remember." Remember! Why, that was the very thing that he didn't want to do. Oh, if only he could forget! But that was what tortured him most. Of course he remembered. He remembered his former life, his life of ease and comfort. He recalled all the good things he had once enjoyed. He remembered his days of prosperity, his lovely home, his large bank account, his rich food. He remembered, too, the cool refreshing breeze and the cold days and nights when he enjoyed the warmth of a fire.

Yes, and he remembered the beggar, lying at his door, and even the stray dogs. He could see them now as they fought over the crumbs that fell from his table and then turned to lick the nauseating sores that covered the skeleton form of Lazarus. How he wished he could forget! But he had to remember.

You, too, will remember. That is what will make Hell really Hell. You will remember your sins; they will haunt you, every one. Those deeds done in secret—you will never, never forget them. You will remember the girl you ruined and damned, the little child you abused, your wasted money, and, worse still, your wasted life. You will remember the many times you heard the Gospel and the times you rejected the invitation to accept Christ. You will recall how the preacher pleaded with you and how you left the meeting unsaved.

But that is not the end of the answer. Abraham has more to say yet. He points out that the situation has been reversed, that the rich man, who had enjoyed the good things of life, is now tormented, and that Lazarus, who had known nothing but suffering, is now comforted. Then he continues:

"And beside all this, between us and you there is a great gulf fixed: so that they who would pass from hence to you cannot; neither can they pass to us, who would come from thence."

What does he say? What new revelation is this? A gulf. Something between. Two things about it.

First, it is a *"great"* gulf. I think of the Grand Canyon. To me *it* is a great gulf, yet it might be possible to find a way to cross it. But not this gulf. It is so wide that no one can cross it. It is a *great* gulf. That means eternal separation. That was why the rich man saw Abraham "afar off". He had landed on the wrong side of the gulf and there he had to stay. "In the place where the tree falleth, there it shall be." There can be no crossing over. Destiny is fixed and fixed for all eternity.

The Bible says that the gulf is too great to cross, that no one on the other side can ever get over, that there is no way to bridge the chasm. No second chance! No opportunity of being saved hereafter. The rich man is still there. He has been there for some two thousand years, and there he will remain. He can never, never cross to where Lazarus is. Oh, my friend, beware lest you, too, land on the wrong side, for if you do you will never get over. It is a *GREAT* gulf.

This means that no one can be prayed out once he is in. Buy all the indulgences you like, pay the priest as much money as you can, have prayers offered by the Church and even by the Pope himself, and all will avail you nothing. Abraham says the gulf can never be crossed. You cannot get anyone out.

Second, it is *"fixed"*: in other words, it can never be removed. The Grand Canyon has been there for thousands of years. This gulf remains forever. It will never disappear. Millennium upon millennium will come and go, but the gulf will still be there. The saved and the lost will never be united. They will always remain apart. The gulf *is fixed*.

His Second Petition

Now for his second petition. Realizing that his own condition is hopeless, he begins to think of others. And thus he prays:

"I pray thee therefore, father, that thou wouldest send him to my father's house: for I have five brethren; that he may testify unto them, lest they also come into this place of torment."

Now it is a good thing to be concerned about one's relatives, but why wasn't he concerned before? Why didn't he speak to them when he had the opportunity? Why leave it so late?

Are we concerned? Do we pray for our relatives now? Or are we, too, going to leave it until it is too late? Perhaps you are not saved yourself and you know you are going to Hell. Tell me, do you want your wife to go with you? Do you want your children to suffer as you will suffer? Have you no burden for those you love? My friend, you had better get anxious now; it will be too late then.

So he prays for his brothers. But now what is Abraham's answer? Marvellous indeed! Listen to it.

"They have Moses and the prophets; let them hear them."

Brief, was it not? Yes, brief indeed, but right to the point. In other words, he said this: "They have the Bible. They have the Word of God. They have the God-breathed writings of Moses and the prophets. Let them hear them."

Oh, the value he places on the Bible! How he honours the Word! It, he says, is all-sufficient. If they will not listen to the voice of God through His prophets, they will not listen to Lazarus. The Word will be their condemnation.

My friend, you have the Word. If you haven't you can get it. Bibles, Testaments and Gospels are sold and even distributed free of charge in countless millions. What more do you need? "Faith cometh by hearing, and hearing by the Word of God."

His Third Petition

But not yet is he through, for he is desperate. For himself he knows there is no hope—but oh, those brothers of his—can he not do something for them? He makes one last attempt. He prays once more. Here is his final petition.

"Nay, father Abraham: but if one went unto them from the dead, they will repent."

What desperation! "If one went unto them from the dead." If a miracle could be wrought. If a dead man could be raised. That's it. Let there be a resurrection, something to startle them. "Raise Lazarus and send him to them." Thus he argued and thus he prayed.

Now for Abraham's last words, his final answer:

"If they hear not Moses and the prophets, neither will they be persuaded though one rise from the dead" (Luke 16: 19–31).

A lot of people think that miracles would convince men. But miracles, my friends, only harden. There was another Lazarus who was raised from the dead, raised after he had been dead four days. Were the rulers convinced? Did that miracle soften their hard hearts? You know it did not.

Again Abraham's only answer is the Word of God. It, and it alone, must suffice. If men will not be convinced and saved through it, there is no hope for them. "If they hear not Moses and the prophets", if they reject the Old Testament Scriptures, they must perish. A miracle would not help.

Not another word is spoken. The rich man is silenced. He has offered his last prayer and now, in horror, he must await the coming of his five brothers, one after the other, unless they repent. The curtain falls and all is over. Ah, but is it? Where is he now? What does he think today?

My friend, you have a choice to make. You can choose to spend Eternity with Lazarus or you can go on as you are and finally go to that place of "torments" to which the rich man went. It is for you to decide.

Will you, then, hear the Word of God and open your heart to Jesus Christ, or will you perish in your sin? Will you be "carried by the angels" to your Home on high, or will you be "buried, and in hell lift up" your "eyes, being in torments"? Which is it to be?

Perhaps you, too, have prayed to a saint. If that saint was Saint Abraham, he would point you to the Word of God. He would say to you in the words of Paul: "Put your trust in the Lord Jesus, and you will be saved." Will you do it? Do it and do it—*NOW*.

CHAPTER XI

THE MADHOUSE OF THE UNIVERSE

WHEN I was a boy I saw a sight that I never can forget—a man carried out of his house in a sheet, in the dead of night. I was watching from an upper window and I was told that the man had gone insane and that he was being taken to a lunatic asylum. Never will I forget the impression it made upon me. I can still remember it.

It may be that there are those in this audience who have had loved ones put away in an asylum, and if so then you know something about it. Death would have been preferable. Perhaps even now you are thinking of a dear one who will have to spend the remainder of his days in such an institution.

We must have asylums to safeguard society. The sane and the insane cannot mix. They simply must be kept apart. For the sake and safety of the sane the insane must be put away.

Now God has an asylum. He, too, knows that the sane and the insane could never be happy together, and so in His asylum—which, by the way, was never prepared for man—the insane will one day have to be put. His asylum was made for the devil and his angels; but since it is the only one He has, therefore the spiritually insane have to be sent to it.

Have you ever visited an asylum? Have you ever seen the insane? I have. One sits thinking, thinking. Another continually weeps. Others wail aloud and gnash their teeth. Their brains have been deranged. They are not themselves. Hence they suffer, suffer in an indescribable way, and there is very little that can be done for them.

God's asylum is called Gehenna, and it is mentioned twelve times in the New Testament Scriptures: eleven times by Christ Himself and once by James. John calls it the Lake of Fire and the Second Death. I have called it the Madhouse of the Universe.

This asylum is a place of conscious suffering. Such words as fire, weeping, wailing, the gnashing of teeth, are used to describe it. Fire burns. People do not weep when they are happy, nor do they wail unless they are miserable. When they gnash their teeth they must be suffering real pain.

So terrible is it that Jesus recommended the loss of hand, foot and eye in preference to being consigned to it.

God Does not Want You to Go There

Let me make it clear, however, that God does not want you to go there.

First of all, it is not His will that *any* should perish. He Himself says so. "Not willing that any should perish" (2 Pet. 3: 9). Hence if you perish and have to be consigned to the asylum prepared for the devil and his angels it will be your own fault. It is not the will of God.

In the second place, God has provided deliverance for you. He has redeemed all mankind. Salvation may be yours; there is no reason, then, why you should ever be consigned to the Madhouse of the Universe. "Christ . . . is the propitiation for . . . the sins of the whole world" (1 John 2: 12).

In the third place, let me point out that He urges you to be saved. "Be ye reconciled to God" (2 Cor. 5: 20).

Again and again throughout the Scriptures He pleads with you to be reconciled. Hence it is not His plan to put you in the asylum that was never prepared for you, but if you refuse to be saved He has no alternative but to send you there.

Who are the Insane?

Now who are the insane? That is the important question; and I want to make three suggestions, if I may, so that you can decide whether or not *you* are insane.

First of all, the Man is Insane who Prepares for the Present and Not the Future

You remember the rich fool. He stored up his grain in his barns; he made an abundant provision for the present; he felt satisfied that he had all that he needed for the rest of his life, and yet God pronounced him a fool; God called him a lunatic, and told him that that very night his soul would be required of him. Why was he insane? Not because he was wealthy, not because he had worked hard, not because he had saved; but because he had made no preparation for the future. The preparation he made was for the present. He gave no thought to his soul. His only thought was for his body. Hence God pronounced him a lunatic. That man was headed for the asylum—the Madhouse of the Universe.

Second, the Man is Insane who Rejects God's Plan and Manufactures One of his Own

God has provided for man's salvation. There is no other way of escape. God gave His Son to die on Calvary's cross and to bear your sins in order that you might not have to bear them. If you reject God's plan and manufacture one of your own, whether it be one of works or religion, or anything else, you are most assuredly insane. Why not accept the God-provided plan? Why try to invent one of your own?

Do you really think that your plan is better than God's? Have you an idea that you can become so religious that you can escape God's asylum? Or do you think that by living a good life you can become sane and thus never have to be consigned to the Madhouse of the Universe? Away with such a thought! God is not going to allow you to substitute your plan for His. There is no other way. You must come through Christ as a poor, helpless, hell-deserving sinner, or not at all.

Third, the Man is Insane who Puts Off his Salvation until his Death-bed

I know the thief was saved on the cross just before he died, but may I point out that the other thief was not? Therefore you are taking a terrible chance. I do not believe the thief ever had another chance. Probably the first time he met the Lord Jesus Christ was when he saw Him hanging by his side on the accursed tree. But you have heard the message again and again. Time after time God's servants have pleaded with you to be reconciled to God and yet you have gone on in your rebellion and rejection, refusing God's offer of mercy.

You have an idea that you can accept Jesus Christ on your death-bed. I would not take that chance for all the world. It has been my privilege to visit a great many of my parishioners who have passed on into the other life, and I want to bear testimony to the fact that in most cases they were far too weak at the end to even think about making a decision for the Lord Jesus Christ. Many who are dying are kept under drugs; their minds are confused;

they cannot think aright. How, then, can they make such a momentous decision?

My friend, any moment you may be cut off. Little did the rich fool think that he would be called to an account that very night. On every side we are surrounded by accidents. In this mechanized world the newspaper is simply filled with reports of accidental deaths. Are you going to take a chance? You are insane if you do; and if you should be cut off without warning, remember—you will go to the Madhouse of the Universe.

These, then, are the men and the women who are insane; and if they are insane now, and if they die in their insanity, what can God do but assign them to His asylum, where all must go who are spiritually insane? It would be impossible for God to allow them to associate with those who are spiritually sane. They would have nothing in common with them. Hence he has to separate them, and the only plan He has is to send them to Gehenna, the place we call Hell, where the devil and his angels are to be consigned, there to be eternally separated from those who have accepted Jesus Christ and are therefore sane in the sight of God.

So Shall It Be

Jesus speaks of the tares being gathered and burned in the fire, and then He says, "So shall it be in the end of this world", or, as it is in the original, "at the end of this age". He Himself will send forth His angels. They are the only ones who can distinguish the sane from the insane. First of all they gather out of His Kingdom all that offend and those who practise iniquity. They will be cast into a furnace of fire, namely, God's asylum, the Madhouse of the Universe, and there the Lord says, "there shall be wailing and gnashing of teeth".

After that He tells us about the sane, and He calls the

sane the righteous. He says that they are to shine forth as the sun in the Kingdom of their Father. The great division has taken place. The insane have been separated from the sane, and now those, by God pronounced sane, are to dwell together, shining as the sun through all the countless ages of eternity.

My friend, to which group do you belong? Are you sane or insane? Will you spend your eternity with the sane in the Kingdom of God, or will you be consigned to the Madhouse of the Universe? It is for you to say.

There was once a young girl who wanted to be saved, but her father said, "If my daughter goes to that altar I will wade in blood to take her out of there." She did not go. Later she became seriously ill and God started to deal with her. Suddenly she cried aloud, "My doom is sealed forever." Then, "What time is it?" Her father told her that it was four o'clock. "Just think," she said, "I am going where there is no time." A moment later she spoke again. "Father," she cried, "get me a drink from the old well, for I am going where there is no water."

A little later she spoke once more. "Father," she said, "put your arms under me and pull me up. My feet are on fire. My feet are slipping. Take my feet out of the fire." After thus agonizing, she again requested, "Bring your daughter another drink of water." He started to get it, but before he got back his beautiful daughter had gone into eternity.

The Choice is Yours

But why say more? The whole world is insane and is bound for the Madhouse of the Universe. Only those who open their hearts to the Lord Jesus Christ and accept Him as a personal Saviour ever become sane. It is for you to decide your own destiny. Are you going to spend it with the sane or with the insane, with the children of God or with the children of Satan, saved or lost, in Heaven above or in the Madhouse of the Universe?

If you refuse, you are insane and you do not want to become sane. You are determined to spend your Eternity in the Madhouse of the Universe rather than in the Paradise of God. You prefer the company of the insane to the company of the sane. And yet you need not go to the Madhouse of the Universe. The resurrected, living Christ can deliver you. The Bible says, "Put your trust in the Lord Jesus, and you will be saved" (Acts 16: 31—N.E.B.). Will you do it? Do it and do it—NOW.

CHAPTER XII

THE BOOK OF REVELATION

I T IS the general consensus of opinion among prophetic students that we are rapidly nearing that period in the world's history commonly known as the End-Time. Perhaps we are already at the threshold of a new order. Certain it is that the Church Age is fast drawing to a close. The Times of the Gentiles have almost run out. Soon, now, the events so long predicted must take place.

But just what will happen? And how soon may we expect the great change? Are the facts given? Can we know for certain? Is there any answer? Thank God, there is! And we turn now to Revelation, the last book in the Bible, generally known as the Apocalypse. For here is prophecy, prophecy in fulfilment, and for the End-Time of the Age.

Seven Observations.

First of all, I want to point out that the visions of the Apocalypse will be perfectly clear to those who will be living in the time of their fulfilment. The wise, as Daniel says, will understand. The book of Revelation is written for the End-Time of the Age. It will be of untold comfort to the saints of that period.

Second—Revelation is the only book in the Bible that has associated with it a special promise of blessing, a blessing to the reader, the hearer and the keeper. You will find it in the third verse of the first chapter. "Blessed is he that *readeth*, and they that *hear* the words of this prophecy, and *keep* those things which are written therein" (Rev. 1: 3). So let us read and hear, let us keep and do, that the blessing promised may be ours.

Then, too, this book carries with it not only a blessing but also a curse. Listen to this from the last chapter, verses eighteen and nineteen. "For I testify unto every man that heareth the words of the prophecy of this book. If any man shall add unto these things, God shall add unto him the plagues that are written in this book: and if any man shall take away from the words of the book of this prophecy, God shall take away his part out of the book of life, and out of the holy city, and from the things which are written in this book." So it behoves us to be on our guard in dealing with Revelation.

Third—I want to point out that the content of Revelation has to do not with Grace but with Judgment, and hence that there is no possibility of its fulfilment during the Church Age, or the present dispensation. God is not now dealing in Judgment, but in Grace.

For that reason above all others, I absolutely reject the historical interpretation, which finds the fulfilment of Revelation in the historical events of the past 1,900 years. So utterly impossible is this interpretation that I need not even comment on it. This is the day of Salvation. God is not now pouring out His judgments. Men may even blaspheme and defy Him, and, for the most part, He remains silent. It will not be so during the dispensation of Judgment.

Fourth—To the casual reader the book of Revelation seems like a tapestry in which scenes are thrown together in a sort of patchwork way, but such is not the case. There is a definite, chronological sequence of events that follow each other in perfect order.

But, like every historian, when some special personage comes on the scene of action or some unusual scene is depicted, the writer pauses, as it were, long enough to describe in detail what he sees, after which he picks up the thread of his narrative and goes on as before.

Hence there are portions of the book of Revelation which are placed in parenthesis, namely, bracketed off from the main line of events. These must first of all be omitted if we are to intelligently grasp our subject, and our attention focused, at the commencement, on the chronological order of things, uninterrupted by the bracketed portions.

Fifth—In order to really understand the Apocalypse we must somewhere find a key that will unlock its message. The question arises: Did Jesus Christ, who on the isle of Patmos gave to His servant John the Revelation, ever before tell the story? He did. While here upon earth, on the Mount of Olives, to His own disciples, some 1,900 years ago, He unfolded, in brief, the whole story of the End-Time. It is found in the twenty-fourth chapter of Matthew's Gospel.

Hence, if the story was told by the same person, and that person Jesus Christ the Son of God, and if it has to do with the same events, then it must coincide. And that is exactly what it does. It was first told when He was in the flesh. It was next told after His resurrection and ascension.

Hence Matthew 24 becomes the key that unlocks the book of Revelation. And what is found in Matthew 24 in epitome is found in Revelation in extended review.

Sixth—Now there is another fact that must be kept in mind, namely, that under the opening of the seventh seal, instead of having what might be expected, a concrete event, we have the blowing of the seven trumpets, which means that everything happening under the seven trumpets belongs to the seventh seal. Thus the seventh seal is extended right through to the end of the seven trumpets.

Then, under the blowing of the seventh trumpet we have the pouring out of the seven vials, so that the seventh trumpet extends to the close of all seven vials. In other words, the seven seals cover the entire period of the last seven years of the Age, commencing with the reign of the Antichrist and closing with the Advent of Christ. The seven trumpets likewise close with the Advent of Christ, and also the seven vials.

The seven trumpets, however, do not commence until the Great Tribulation has practically ended, or at least is drawing to a close, and the seven vials are poured out immediately at the end of the Tribulation period. So that while four of the seals *precede* the Tribulation, and the fifth seal *is* the Tribulation, the seven trumpets and vials all *close the* Tribulation.

The seven seals are the happenings under the reign of the Antichrist before and during the Great Tribulation. The seven trumpets, on the other hand, are the judgments of God upon an unbelieving world. The first four are mild in comparison to the others; so much so that the last three are called "woes". And as a result of the first woe, which is the fifth trumpet, for the first time men suffer and yet are denied death; whereas when the sixth trumpet is blown one-third of the human race die. Hence there is an increase and an intensity of judgment.

Now whereas the trumpets are the judgments of God, the vials constitute the wrath of God. They are brief but terrible, and immediately upon the pouring out of the seventh vial we have the statement: "It is done." So that the wrath of the Antichrist under the fifth seal, the judgments of God under the trumpets, and His wrath under the vials, are all completed. Consequently, in the nineteenth chapter we are ready for the battle of Armageddon, and the Second Advent.

Then follows the destruction of the Antichrist, the False Prophet and his armies, the binding of Satan, the ushering in of the Millennium, with Christ reigning on David's throne for a thousand years, the release of Satan for a short period, his final doom, and the judgment of the Great White Throne, culminating in the creation of the new heavens and the new earth wherein dwelleth righteousness.

The Throne in Heaven.

Revelation divides itself into three major sections, each stated in verse seventeen of the first chapter. "Write the things which thou hast seen," namely, the past, "and the things which are," the present, "and the things which shall be hereafter," the future. Chapter one covers the past, chapters two and three, the present, and from chapter four to the end of the book, the future.

According to verse nine of chapter one John had been exiled to Patmos for his faith in Christ. There he receives the vision. Perhaps the key verse to the entire book is verse seven of chapter one: "Behold, He cometh with clouds; and every eye shall see Him, and they also which pierced Him: and all kindreds of the earth shall wail because of Him." For the Apocalypse is the unveiling of Jesus Christ in connection with His Second Advent.

John is shown a throne in Heaven, God's throne. It is surrounded by twenty-four elders, all clothed in white, and with crowns of gold on their heads. Lightnings, thunderings and voices proceed from the throne. Seven lamps burn before it. In the midst are four living creatures, in the authorized version translated "beasts". And before the throne is a sea of glass.

Day and night the four living creatures worship and praise God. "Holy, holy, holy, Lord God Almighty, which was, which is, and is to come," they cry in unison. And as they thus praise him "who liveth for ever and ever, the twenty-four elders fall down and worship, and cast their crowns before the throne," exclaiming, "Thou art worthy, O Lord, to receive glory and honour and power: for thou hast created all things, and for thy pleasure they are and were created."

What a magnificent spectacle! Isn't it glorious to realize that amid the toppling thrones of earth there is a throne "set", namely, established, one throne that can never fall! How secure and safe is the kingdom, therefore, of which that throne is the centre. There is one stable government, at least.

Now the scene changes. It is still in Heaven and before the throne, but a book appears, and an angel cries aloud for someone who is worthy to open it. No one answers and John commences to weep. Then an elder informs him that Jesus Christ is able to loose the seals and bids him weep no more. A Lamb appears, a Lamb that had been slain. He, the Lord Jesus Christ, takes the book from the hand of God.

Immediately the elders and living creatures fall down before Him and together sing the new song: "Thou art worthy to take the book, and to open the seals thereof: for Thou wast slain and hast redeemed us by Thy blood out of every kindred and tongue and people and nation; and hast made us unto our God kings and priests: and we shall reign on the earth." So that the Lamb is none other than Christ Himself, for He alone is the Redeemer.

Then, myriads of angels appear, "ten thousand times ten thousand, and thousands of thousands," so the record reads. What a multitude! "Worthy is the Lamb that was slain to receive power, and riches, and wisdom, and strength, and honour, and glory, and blessing, they sing together. What a choir! Surely mortal man never heard the like before. To picture the majesty of the scene is beyond the power of human language. It is glory indescribable.

The vision closes with a universal exclamation of adoration and worship to both Father and Son: "Blessing, and honour, and glory, and power, be unto Him that sitteth upon the throne, and unto the Lamb forever and ever."

The Seven Seals.

Let us bear in mind that the opening of the first four seals takes place previous to the Tribulation, as already stated, and that these are therefore the pre-Tribulation seals. The four horsemen presented to us clearly indicate restlessness, activity, turmoil, for a horse is never used in the Scriptures to denote peace.

The first is white. Here we have the Antichrist, or the false messiah, who rides forth at the beginning of the last seven years of the age, namely, the seventieth week of Daniel, to commence his diabolical reign, conquering and to conquer. He heads up the revived Roman Empire, overcomes three of the ten kings who rise against him, and establishes himself as head over the remaining seven, thus bringing the entire world into subjection to him.

The red horse, in verses three and four, denotes war, and this is in perfect agreement with Matthew 24. There can be no peace under the reign of the Antichrist apart from the peace of subjection. Hence his reign is immediately followed by bloodshed.

The black horse, in verses five and six, represents famine, and the pale horse, in verses seven and eight, pestilence or death. Yet all these, terrible though they are, are only the beginnings of travail, and, occurring in the first three and a half years, they but usher in the Great Tribulation, when the real tragedy of suffering commences.

Hence, under the opening of the fifth seal, in verses nine to eleven, we have presented the Great Tribulation commencing with the middle of the seventieth week of Daniel, and coinciding exactly with the setting in Matthew 24. Many are martyred, and, as in the imprecatory Psalms, the victims cry for vengeance, but are told to rest a little while until more martyrs are added to their number, for the end of the Tribulation is not yet.

Under the sixth seal the sun and the moon become darkened, which is in perfect agreement with Acts, chapter two, verse twenty: "The sun shall be turned into darkness and the moon into blood before that great and notable day of the Lord come." And it will be remembered that the same darkening of sun and moon is described as following the Tribulation, in Matthew's Gospel, so that each event is in perfect order.

This seal brings us to the immediate Coming of Christ in power and glory, to the time when men will hide themselves in the dens and rocks, crying, "Fall on us, and hide us from the face of Him that sitteth on the throne, and from the wrath of the Lamb: for the great day of His wrath is come." Hence we are prepared for the manifestation of God's wrath and the events immediately connected with the Second Advent itself.

The Seven Trumpets.

Passing over chapter seven, which is in parenthesis and does not belong to the general order of events, we take up the narrative again at chapter eight, where we have the sounding of the seven trumpets. In the first verse the seventh seal is opened, and, as previously stated, instead of a single event, we have, under this seal, the sounding of all seven trumpets.

These trumpets, it will be remembered, constitute the judgments of God, and they are sounded at approximately the close of the tribulation period. The Antichrist has now reigned for almost seven years. The time of his doom is at hand, but before he himself is dealt with, the unbelieving world is visited by the judgments of Almighty God.

The first trumpet, in verse seven, destroys a third part of the trees and all the green grass. The second, in verses eight and nine, turns the third part of the sea into blood and destroys a third part of sea life and ships. The third trumpet, in verse ten, makes a third of the waters bitter and results in the death of many who dare to drink of them. The fourth trumpet, in verse twelve, darkens a third part of the sun, moon and stars, and reminds us of the similar plague wrought by Moses in Egypt.

At this point there is a definite break in the soundings of the trumpets, and an angel appears, flying through the heavens and crying: "Woe, woe, woe, to the inhabiters of the earth by reason of the other voices of the trumpets of the three angels, which are yet to sound!" The reason is not far to seek. The first four judgments are mild, terrible though they are, in comparison with the three yet to follow. Moreover, they have to do with physical nature alone, whereas the others have to do with men. So terrible are these last three that they are designated the "woe" trumpets.

When the fifth trumpet is sounded, which is the first woe, the bottomless pit is opened, namely, the abyss, and hordes of demons, called locusts, with the power of scorpions, are loosed. They are organized and have a king over them. They are forbidden to hurt the grass or anything green, including trees, but are commanded to attack and torment all men who have not the seal of God in their

foreheads. Yet their power is limited; they are not permitted to kill, but only to cause indescribable suffering
for a period of five months. So terrible will be the agony
that men will seek death, but will find it impossible to
die.

Now, when the sixth trumpet is sounded, the angels
loosed have almost unlimited power, even to the extent
of death, and are permitted to destroy men; so that, as
a result of their judgment, one-third are slain. The entire
army numbers 200,000,000, a multitude beyond our
imagination. The destructive work is done, not by the
riders on the horses, but by the horses themselves.

Omitting chapter ten, which is in parenthesis, and the
first part of chapter eleven, we continue the second woe at
the thirteenth verse, thus closing up the sounding of the
fifth trumpet. A great earthquake destroys a tenth part
of the city and slays seven thousand men. So terrible is
it that, for the first time, those escaping the catastrophe
are filled with fear, and acknowledge that God's hand is
in it.

The third woe follows quickly as the seventh trumpet
is sounded; and once again we are brought right up to the
return of our Lord. "The kingdoms of this world are
become the kingdoms of our Lord and of His Christ;
and He shall reign for ever and ever." Thus we have
again the announcement of God's wrath (verse 18), the
time of the judging of the dead and the giving of rewards
to the faithful, ending with the destruction of those in
opposition.

The Seven Vials.

We must now omit chapters twelve to fifteen, except to
note verses six and seven of chapter fifteen, where it is
announced that the angels with the seven plagues appear,

and are ready to pour out their vials full of the wrath of God on an unbelieving world. In chapter sixteen is presented the actual outpouring, in rapid succession, of these vials. This must occur just prior to the Battle of Armageddon and at the close of the Tribulation period.

It will be noted that the vials, unlike the judgments, fall upon man rather than upon vegetation.

The first strikes all those who have received the mark of the beast and worshipped his image, and takes the form of a grievous sore (16: 2). The second vial, poured upon the sea, destroys every living creature therein. And the third, on the rivers, turns their waters into blood.

That God's judgments are righteous is here admitted. "Thou art righteous, O Lord, for they have shed the blood of saints and prophets and Thou hast given them blood to drink. True and righteous are Thy judgments" (16: 5–7).

The fourth vial, poured upon the sun, increases its heat to such an extent that men are literally scorched: and in this we have the fulfilment of the prophecy concerning the day that is to burn as an oven (Mal. 4: 1; Isa. 24: 6; 42: 25). Yet, instead of repenting, it is plainly stated that "they repented not."

These four vials, it will be noted, affect man in general and culminate in his continued rebellion and insubordination; but when the fifth is poured out, it falls, not on man, but on the seat of the beast, the Antichrist of darkness, and the suffering caused is so great that they gnaw their tongues in pain (verse 10). Yet their only reaction is to blaspheme God and refuse, in spite of their torment, to repent (verse 11).

Now, having dealt with man in general, as the first four vials are poured out, and with the Antichrist in particular through the fifth vial, God turns to the preparation that must be made for the Battle of Armageddon and the final overthrow of the Antichrist. The sixth vial, therefore, affects the river Euphrates, dries up its waters, and makes a road for the kings of the East, with their armies.

Verses thirteen to sixteen are in parenthesis, so that we omit them and take up the thread of our story again at verse seventeen. Until now the vials have affected only the earth, the rivers, and seas, and all that dwell on the earth or live in the waters, except the fourth, which had to do with the sun; but thus far the air has remained untouched. The seventh, however, has to do with the atmosphere itself. Voices, thunders and lightnings are heard and seen; but most prominent of all are two outstanding catastrophes, namely, an earthquake and a hailstorm.

The earthquake is the worst ever experienced in the history of the world. It results in the overthrow of all the cities of the earth, with the exception of Jerusalem, which is divided into three parts. Babylon, possibly a literal re-built city, but probably Rome, the civic seat of the Antichrist, suffers most, the judgment consisting of the cup of the wine of the fierceness of the wrath of God. Even the islands disappear, and the mountains are levelled on every side. What a catastrophe!

But this is not all. In addition to the earthquake there is a hailstorm unprecedented in violence. Each stone, it is stated, weighs eighty-five pounds. And these hailstones fall upon those still remaining, who have rebelled against God. It reminds us of the hailstorm of Egypt through the agency of Moses. Yet, once again, punishment fails to produce repentance, for men still blaspheme God in spite of all their sufferings.

Most significant are three words occurring in the seventeenth verse, namely, "It is done." God has sent His judgments under the seven trumpets, and poured out His wrath under the seven vials, and now the exact End is reached. It is time for the final test in the Battle of Armageddon, the Advent of His Son, and the establishment of the Millennium. Hence the exclamation: "It is done." At last, the long, dark Age is brought to a close, and the dawn of a New appears on the horizon.

The Second Advent and the Millennium.

Passing over chapters seventeen, eighteen and nineteen down to verse ten, all of which is in parenthesis, and taking up the order of events again at verse eleven in chapter nineteen, we are brought immediately to the Second Coming of Christ in power and glory. Like the false messiah of chapter six, who appeared on a white horse, the true now rides forth to complete the subjection of His kingdom, and to establish His millennial reign.

"And I saw Heaven opened, and behold a white horse; and He that sat upon him was called Faithful and True, and in righteousness He doth judge and make war. His eyes were as a flame of fire, and on His head were many crowns; and He had a name written, that no man knew but He Himself. And He was clothed with a vesture dipped in blood: and His name is called The Word of God.

"And the armies which were in Heaven followed Him upon white horses, clothed in fine linen, white and clean. And out of His mouth goeth a sharp sword, that with it He should smite the nations: and He shall rule them with a rod of iron; and He treadeth the winepress of the fierceness and wrath of Almighty God. And He hath on his vesture and on His thigh a name written, KING OF KINGS, AND LORD OF LORDS."

Thus He rides forth, and for the first time in the history of the world, judgment in righteousness is meted out. Accompanied by the armies of Heaven, He comes, all on white horses, symbolic of power and authority; and with a rod of iron He rules the smitten nations. No mistaking His identity; our Saviour is at last recognized and acknowledged as King of kings and Lord of lords.

Who can describe the majesty, the splendour of His Appearance! What a revelation to a rebellious world! After an absence of some 2,000 years, at last the silence is broken, and God intervenes once more. What a joy to the scattered remnant! How earnestly they had prayed and waited, watching daily for the opening in the skies! Day after day had gone by, and still He tarried. Their darkest night had come; but lo! the dawn, though little they knew it, was at hand.

Suddenly, as they watch, beset on every side by the Antichrist and his armies, their attention is focused on a most extraordinary phenomenon in the skies—the Heavens open, the clouds part, and lo! a Figure, clad in brightness that outshines the sun, suddenly appears. Thousands upon thousands circle round him, angels and archangels, the vast armies of Heaven, and, in addition, innumerable saints who had been raptured away.

What a sight!—earth's long-lost Messiah at last returning, returning in all His regal splendour, Lord of lords and King of kings.

The Battle of Armageddon has been fought and, apparently, won by the Antichrist and his armies. Revelation, seventeen to nineteen, tells the story. For the Antichrist, the kings under him and their armies, having defeated the remnant of the Jews, are now gathered, daring to make war with the Lord Himself. And, knowing the result, the fowls of the air are invited to feast themselves on the carcasses of the slain.

Swift and sure is the outcome. Verse twenty most graphically sums it up. The Antichrist is taken, captured alive. Also the False Prophet, who through his miracles had deceived the nations, especially the worshippers of the image, the recipients of the mark of the beast. Even death is defeated, for they are cast, both of them, alive, into the lake of fire that burns with brimstone, and their armies slain. This is not the end of them, however; we shall see them once again.

Now comes the establishment of the Millennium, as set forth in chapter twenty. True, the Antichrist and the False Prophet have been dealt with, but not their leader. Satan is still at large. And before there can be any peace, he must be arrested and imprisoned.

To an angel is given this task, and, with the key of the bottomless pit and a great chain in his hand, he proceeds to arrest the Devil, to bind him with the chain, and to cast him into the bottomless pit, which is then sealed, so that the nations are no longer deceived, at least not for a thousand years, which is the entire period of the Millennium.

For some six thousand years he has been at work as the enemy of souls, seeking to destroy God's Kingdom and to gain control over the hearts and lives of His saints. For one thousand years at least his diabolical work will cease, and his temptations be no more. With Satan at large, there can be no Millennium; but with Satan bound, the Golden Age will be a glorious reality.

Commencing with verse four, we are brought face to face with the majestic vision of the Millennium in its initial stage. Thrones appear, each one occupied; many by the martyrs, especially those who had refused to worship the Antichrist and his image, or to receive his mark. These, it is stated, lived; that is, lived in resurrection, and reigned with Christ a thousand years. Thus the kingdom is established, with the Lord Jesus Christ and those of His followers who have qualified, reigning in millennial splendour.

H

But there is another company. They are called "the rest of the dead," namely, the unsaved of all ages. These are not resurrected at the beginning of the Millennium. In fact, they remain in their graves until the close of that wonderful period. "This," the writer says, referring back to those who live and reign with Christ, "is the *first resurrection*." And then he goes on to speak of the blessedness of these who share it; the first blessing being that they will never be compelled to endure "the second death"; the next, that "they shall be priests of God and of Christ"; and the third, that "they shall reign with Him a thousand years."

Thus it is obvious that there is a vast difference in Eternity between the saved and the lost; and it is quite evident even now to all those who read these verses, that they need not wait until some future day to know their destiny. Either they will be alive for a thousand years, or, during the same period, their bodies will be in the grave, and they themselves in the place of departed spirits; for these two resurrections lie a thousand years apart.

Are you, my friend, to be numbered with the first group or with the second? Where will you be during the Millennium? In which resurrection will you rise? Remember that to be born once is to die twice, but to be born twice is to die once, and not at all if Christ should come first. The choice rests with you.

The Final Revolt.

Now comes the final revolt. Satan is loosed from his prison. For one thousand years he has been in captivity. The bottomless pit has held him fast. In verse three we have the statement: "After that he must be loosed a little season." Thank God, it is but for "a little season," a short time. In verse seven it is stated "that when the thousand years are expired Satan shall be loosed out of his prison."

Once again, filled with rage, he sallies forth to gather together the nations, the nations from whence had come the armies that followed the Antichrist, the nations over which Christ had ruled with a rod of iron for a thousand years. So vast is the army that it is compared to the sand of the sea.

Around the camp of the saints they gather, namely, around Jerusalem, the beloved city, eager to overthrow the government of the Lord Jesus Christ, and place Satan, their leader, on the throne. It is the last great attempt to wrench the sceptre from the Son of God, and it fails.

The battle is of short duration. God, Himself, accomplishes the overthrow, for fire comes down out of heaven, and the vast armies of the Devil are completely and forever destroyed.

Now follows the final downfall of Satan himself, as set forth in verse ten. At last his career is ended. He will deceive no more. At the close of his insurrection he finds himself in the lake of fire and brimstone.

But he is not alone. Those, through whom he carried on his hellish work, are there to welcome him. The Antichrist and the False Prophet, who for a thousand years have endured the lake of fire, are still there. And now it is stated that "he shall be tormented day and night for ever and ever."

The Great White Throne.

Commencing with verse eleven of chapter twenty, we have the vivid description of the Great White Throne Judgment. It is the next act in the drama. The dead, small and great, stand before God. Not the saved, for they were raised a thousand years previously and have been living and reigning with Christ for centuries. These dead comprise only the lost, those who through ages past have rejected the Lord Jesus Christ. They, too, are now resurrected and sentence is passed upon them. Not one escapes.

From the place of departed spirits they return, a great multitude. Their doom is the lake of fire. "This is the second death." Verse fifteen says "whosoever". How vividly it reminds us of that other "whosoever" in John 3: 16. There are only the two great companies, namely, "whosoever believeth in Him," and "whosoever was not found written in the Book of Life". And of these latter it is said that they "are cast into the lake of fire".

The Two Companies.

Having now disposed of the various events prophesied in Revelation in their chronological order, we continue our study by going back to the passages in parenthesis, which we omitted. And first of all the two companies in chapter seven.

An angel, described as ascending from the east with the seal of God, cries, with a loud voice, to the four angels who, presumably, will sound the first four trumpets, "Hurt not the earth, neither the sea, nor the trees, till we have sealed the servants of our God in their foreheads." The first four trumpet judgments, it will be remembered, affected the trees, the grass, the sea, sea-life, ships, the rivers, the sun, the moon, and the stars, and to protect God's servants in the midst of these calamities, this angel is sent.

Two groups are seen, the first Jewish and the second Gentile. The first are numbered, namely 144,000, the second are numberless, and are spoken of as "a great multitude which no man could number, of all nations, and kindreds, and people, and tongues." The first are on earth, namely the Jewish company, and the second, the Gentiles, in Heaven.

The first company, apparently, came *through* the Tribulation, but escaped by preservation. The second came *out* of it. "These are they which came out of great tribulation," reads the inspired Record. Hence the Jews in this company are the tribulation saints, and the Gentiles the tribulation martyrs. Obviously, then, there will be many saved during the reign of the Antichrist.

Undoubtedly the group referred to in Revelation fourteen, one to five, is the same. Here the scene is on earth, at Jerusalem. Christ has come. Around Him are gathered 144,000, and, be it noted, His Father's seal is in their foreheads. It is stated of them that they have followed the Lamb wholly, and have lived lives of separation from all defilement. Holiness characterized them while on earth, and they are uncontaminated by the world. Because of their acceptance of God's righteousness, in Jesus Christ, they are without fault, and utterly guileless. They were redeemed from among men, redeemed, of course, by the Blood of the Lord Jesus Christ.

What a scene is presented by the second group, namely, the Gentile multitudes, also saved in the midst of the Tribulation, but martyred for their faith! Evidently God is no respecter of persons, for every nationality is represented. With joyful acclaim, they appear before the throne of God, crying, "Salvation to our God, and unto the Lamb." And, in response, angels, elders, and the four living creatures fall on their faces, and worship God, exclaiming, as with one voice, "Blessing, and glory, and wisdom, and thanksgiving, and honour, and power, and might, be unto our God for ever and ever."

There they stand, arrayed in white robes. "Who are they?" asks one of the elders. "Sir," replies John, "thou knowest." Triumphantly the answer is given, and oh, what a revelation! Who would spurn martyrdom, Who would fear the Great Tribulation? Listen:

"These are they which came out of great tribulation and have washed their robes, and made them white in the blood of the Lamb. Therefore are they before the throne of God, and serve Him day and night in His temple: and He that sitteth on the throne shall dwell among them. They shall hunger no more, neither thirst any more; neither shall the sun light on them, nor any heat. For the Lamb which is in the midst of the throne shall feed them, and shall lead them unto living fountains of waters: and God shall wipe away all tears from their eyes."

The Little Book.

Our next passage in parenthesis is found in chapter ten. A mighty angel appears, clothed with a cloud, a rainbow on his head, his face like the sun, his feet as pillars of fire. In his hand he holds a little book, and it is open. Placing his right foot on the sea, and his left on the earth, he cries aloud, cries with a voice so loud that it sounds to John like a lion's roar. Immediately seven thunders utter their voices, and John commences to write, but is forbidden. Hence, what the thunders said we do not know.

Then the same mighty angel lifts his hand to heaven and swears that the End-Time has come, declaring that during the days in which the seventh angel sounds his trumpet the mystery of God would be finished.

John is then commanded to take the little book and eat it. He does so, and discovers first its sweetness, then its bitterness. The last verse gives us the explanation. The little book is God's message, first with its offer of love and mercy, then of judgment and condemnation. John has yet to prophesy many things.

The Two Witnesses.

Continuing the passages in parenthesis, we turn to chapter eleven, and discover, in verse two, that the Great Tribulation is to last for a period of forty-two months, which, of course, is three and a half years, and that during that time Gentile world power will hold complete sway over Jerusalem.

Now appear the two witnesses. Who they are we know not. Malachi tells us that Elijah is to return before the great day of the Lord (Mal. 4: 5). Verse six would indicate that they have the same power that Moses and Elijah had, for they cause the rainfall to cease, turn the waters into blood, and smite the earth with all manner of plagues. Hence, they may be Moses and Elijah.

God never leaves Himself without witnesses. Even during the days of the Great Tribulation, the darkest period of the world's history, He has His representatives.

They are to prophesy for 1,260 days, which equals approximately forty-two months or, again, three and a half years, namely, the entire period of the Tribulation. Their testimony, be it noted, closes when the sixth trumpet has been sounded, which is the second woe.

They are energized by the Holy Spirit, according to verse four, and are to shine as God's lights in the midst of universal darkness. In all probability, they will proclaim to a deceived and unbelieving world the truth about the Antichrist, and will expose his lies and deceptions, warning men of his coming doom.

God's servants, who live in the centre of His Will, are immortal until their life's work is done. According to verse five, these two witnesses are protected from the wrath of the Antichrist until they have furnished their testimony. Finally, in the midst of the sounding of the sixth trumpet, they are slain, slain by the Antichrist himself; and for three and a half days their bodies lie unburied in the streets of Jerusalem, while all the world rejoices.

But, lo, and behold, at the end of three and a half days, to the amazement of all, they are suddenly resurrected. How surprised the multitudes will be! For three and a half days they had been exchanging gifts. The newspapers, in all probability, had been carrying flaring headlines, and writing triumphant editorials regarding the victory of the world emperor over God's last representatives on earth.

How startled all will be when, suddenly, those two bodies, lying there in the street, move, sit up, and then stand upright on their feet! But they will not have long to watch. Presently a voice from Heaven speaks, and, distinctly, they hear the command, "Come up hither." A moment later, their feet leave the earth, as they ascend in a cloud, while their enemies, multiplied thousands in number, gaze at them.

It will be remembered, in our study of the second woe, we discovered that, in less than an hour after their ascension, a terrible earthquake destroys a tenth part of Jerusalem and takes a toll of seven thousand lives, and that, for the first time, fear clutches at the hearts of men, so much so that they somehow acknowledge God.

The Two Wonders.

The third parenthetical passage presents the two wonders in chapter twelve, and several personages. The woman, Israel, gives birth to the child, Christ, and is pursued by the dragon, Satan. Christ ascends to God.

He is spoken of as the One who is to rule the nations with a rod of iron. It was Isaiah who exclaimed, "Unto us a child is born, unto us a son is given" (Isa. 9: 6). It was Herod who, instigated by Satan, sought to slay the Christ child. Hence the woman's child is Christ.

Soon the scene shifts to the End-Time, and the period of the Great Tribulation, when Satan again pursues the Jews, through the Antichrist. The time is 1,260 days, or forty-two months, *viz.*, three and a half years. God Himself protects His chosen people, and preserves a remnant during the awful years of Jacob's trouble.

At the beginning of the Tribulation, Satan is cast out of the air, on to the earth, with his angels. No longer can he accuse the saints. The heavens rejoice, but to the earth it is woe. Satan, filled with wrath, knowing that his time is short, namely, three and a half years, prepares to do his worst.

Yet, even in that dark hour of persecution, the saints remain true to God, overcoming the Devil, as always, through the merits of the Blood, and by the power of their testimony. Almost recklessly they bear testimony to their Lord, and even rejoice in martyrdom, fearlessly facing the Antichrist himself, for it says that "they loved not their lives unto the death."

The Two Beasts.

Our fourth passage in parenthesis, leads us to the two beasts of Revelation 13, perhaps by all odds the most important chapter in the book. The beast out of the sea is first described in verses one to ten, and is, of course, the Antichrist himself, while the second beast, out of the earth, described in verses eleven to eighteen, is the False Prophet.

The description is self-explanatory. As I have before

pointed out, the Antichrist, in all probability, will be a reincarnation of the world's superman, who will be the head of the revived Roman Empire. He will be assassinated. Into his dead body will come the spirit of a man who lived some two thousand years ago, for he is to come up out of the bottomless pit (11: 7; 13: 3; 17: 8). In every respect, he fulfils the description given by Paul, being guilty of blasphemy, and drawing to himself the worship of all those whose names are not written in the Lamb's Book of Life. He perfectly fits into the picture drawn by Daniel in every respect.

The False Prophet will be the miracle worker. Several of the miracles that he will perform are mentioned. It will be his prerogative to secure universal worship for the Antichrist. Force will, of course, be used. God help His saints when they will be unable either to buy or sell, unless they submit to the mark.

The Six Angels.

Having already dealt with the first five verses of chapter fourteen, we now glance at the remainder of the chapter. Six angels appear. What power God's angels have! And what a part they play in the End-Time drama!

The first angel proclaims the Everlasting Gospel. The second announces the fall of Babylon. The third warns of impending wrath upon all who receive the mark of the beast. The fourth proclaim that earth's harvest is ripe, and commands the one sitting on the cloud to reap. The fifth appears with a sharp sickle. The sixth tells him to thrust in his sickle, and gather the clusters of the vine, stating that the grapes are over-ripe.

The chapter closes with a description of the Battle of Armageddon. It is near the city of Jerusalem, and so terrible is the slaughter, that blood flows to the horses' bridles.

In the midst of the Tribulation, it is stated, according to verse thirteen, that so far as the saints are concerned, death is preferable to life. In other words, it is better to die than to live. Martyrdom is welcomed. Rest and reward are promised. Listen: "Blessed are the dead that die in the Lord from henceforth: yea, saith the Spirit, that they may rest from their labours; and their works do follow them." The emphasis is on the words, "from henceforth," for, during the Tribulation, death by martyrdom will be an escape from untold suffering and a gateway into endless bliss.

In verse two of chapter fifteen, John sees once again the sea of glass, and says that it is mingled with fire, and that those standing on it have been victorious over the Antichrist and have not received his image, his mark or the number of his name. With harps of God in their hands, they sing the song of Moses and the Lamb.

Two companies are seen, the one saved, the other lost; one in Gehenna, the other on the sea of glass before the throne of God. There is no indication that anyone who ever consents to receive the mark of the beast will be saved. Whereas those who refuse his mark, though they may suffer martyrdom, are at last seen in the very presence of God Himself.

Just here there is a short passage in parenthesis, namely, verses thirteen to sixteen of chapter sixteen. The Battle of Armageddon is definitely announced. Innumerable demons sent forth by Satan, the Antichrist and the False Prophet, here called "unclean spirits like frogs," go forth with miracle-working power and incite the kings of earth to war.

Little do these rulers know that they are being persuaded by demons and that the war in which they are so eager to engage will end in the Battle of Armageddon. Little do the nations of our day realize that demon power is responsible for most of the wars that have been fought and will yet be fought.

As a result of the work accomplished by these demons, the armies of the nations are gathered together for the last great battle—Armageddon, which is fought outside the city of Jerusalem, on the plain of Jezreel, in the valley of Megiddo.

The Two Babylons.

There is one last passage, commencing at chapter seventeen, which we have omitted, but it requires only a brief analysis.

The great whore is, of course, apostate Christianity, including Roman Catholicism, the Greek Orthodox Church, and all Protestantism where there has been a departure from the Faith. Perhaps the gigantic system, known as Roman Catholicism, is most in evidence. Rome has assumed a political attitude, has claimed to be superior to all temporal power, and has been guilty of intercourse with various nations of the world.

John sees a woman sitting upon a scarlet-coloured beast, Roman Catholicism is coming back into power, once more, before the final overthrow. Ecclesiastical Babylon is in the saddle. The beast carries the woman, hence Catholicism is supreme. The Roman Empire has been revived, but for the time being, it is dominated by religious Babylon.

Roman Catholicism is the only system fulfilling verses five and six. The Spanish Inquisition, the slaughter of the Huguenots, and the Waldensians, as well as numerous other atrocities, were of Rome's invention.

The procedure for the revival of the Roman Empire is clearly portrayed. Verse twelve tells us that ten kings, who will probably at first be dictators, will arise and amalgamate under the leadership of the Antichrist. These ten, representing civil Babylon, will finally turn on the woman, ecclesiastical Babylon, and utterly destroy her. Hence, Roman Catholicism will, at last, be abolished, and not a vestige remain.

The last verse of the chapter informs us that the woman represents Rome, the only city that has ever reigned over kings as a religious power. Verse fifteen interprets the waters as "peoples, multitudes, nations, and tongues." Roman Catholicism, again, is the only system that has actually dominated nations.

The eighteenth chapter proclaims the fall of Babylon. Two Babylons, of course, are in view, namely, apostate Christendom, which is ecclesiastical Babylon, and is headed up by the papacy, and political Babylon, the final form of Gentile world dominion. Ecclesiastical Babylon is destroyed by political Babylon, and political Babylon by the coming of the Lord Jesus Christ.

At the beginning of chapter nineteen we are told that God, in righteousness, has judged the whore, and avenged the blood of His saints. As a matter of fact, all Heaven is moved, for with one voice, praises ascend to God. Great is the rejoicing of those redeemed. "Salvation, and glory, and honour, and power," they cry, "unto the Lord our God."

The New Heavens and the New Earth.

Glorious beyond expression is the scene depicted in chapter twenty-one, after all the sorrow and sadness of the past. Oh, how the prophet's heart must have thrilled as he beheld the wondrous vision! "I saw a new heaven and a new earth: for the first heaven and the first earth were passed away," he exclaims.

As John gazed on the new earth, his attention was suddenly attracted by the descent of the Holy City, the New Jerusalem, the abode of God Himself, coming down out of Heaven. And, oh, what a city! The description taxes the imagination.

Suffice it to say that, in addition to its precious stones, its gates of pearl and its streets of gold, according to the inspired description, "the city had no need of the sun, neither of the moon, to shine in it: for the glory of God did lighten it, and the Lamb is the light thereof." And so, "there shall be no night there."

The closing chapter of the book pictures "a pure river of water of life, clear as crystal, proceeding out of the throne of God and of the Lamb." It tells us of a tree of life and its twelve manner of fruits, a tree bearing fruit each month.

The book closes with the glorious promises of our Lord's soon return. Verse seven says: "Behold, I come quickly." Verse twelve declares: "And, behold, I come quickly; and my reward is with me, to give every man according as his work shall be." Verse twenty states: "Surely I come quickly." And then John adds, "Even so, come, Lord Jesus."